M000287299

Say It in Spanish!

SAY IT IN SPANISH!
Language and Activities for the Elementary Classroom

Marianne Mitchell

1997
TEACHER IDEAS PRESS
A Division of
Libraries Unlimited, Inc.
Englewood, Colorado

To Jaime
¡muchísimas gracias!

Copyright © 1997 Marianne Mitchell
All Rights Reserved
Printed in the United States of America

No part of this publication may be reproduced, stored in a retrieval system, or transmitted, in any form or by any means, electronic, mechanical, photocopying, recording, or otherwise, without the prior written permission of the publisher. An exception is made for individual library media specialists and teachers, who may make copies of activity sheets for classroom use in a single school. Other portions of the book (up to 15 pages) may be copied for in-service programs or other educational programs in a single school.

TEACHER IDEAS PRESS
A Division of
Libraries Unlimited, Inc.
P.O. Box 6633
Englewood CO 80155-6633
1-800-237-6124

Production Editor: Kay Mariea
Proofreader: Patricia Dubrava Keuning
Design and Layout: Pamela J. Getchell

Library of Congress Cataloging-in-Publication Data

Mitchell, Marianne, 1947-
    Say it in Spanish! : language and activities for the elementary classroom / Marianne Mitchell.
        xi, 122 p. 22x28 cm.
        Includes bibliographical references and index.
        ISBN 1-56308-434-1
        1. Spanish language--Textbooks for foreign speakers--English.
    2. Spanish language--Study and teaching (Elementary)   I. Title.
PC4129.E5M58   1996
468.2'421372--dc20   96-24870
                                                             CIP

CONTENTS

PREFACE

Here you are, facing the challenge of using Spanish in the classsroom. Don't panic! Remember, you don't have to learn *everything* about Spanish. You don't need to know how to order airline tickets, bargain in the market, or write a business letter. All you need to know is: CLASSROOM SPANISH!

This book was created for the elementary teacher who wants to teach Spanish as a second language or to communicate better with Spanish-speaking students and parents. It presents the basics of how to pronounce Spanish so the teacher can (without fear) read a story to the class, give students basic commands, and have fun learning a new language. It also includes vocabulary used in daily classroom routines, such as saying the Pledge of Allegiance, doing the calendar, and talking about the weather. There are games, activities, songs, poems, art projects, and a vocabulary list organized by category. The bibliography suggests some easy books for the beginning Spanish class.

You won't find all there is to know about Spanish here. You will find basic beginning Spanish and the terms you will need for a classroom setting. Grammar, vocabulary, and activities were chosen carefully to avoid being overwhelming or confusing.

Young students don't have the same inhibitions about learning a language that adults do. To them it's a game, like learning a secret code. They are eager to repeat whatever is modeled. If you feel confident about using Spanish, the children will enjoy it, too.

So, relax! This won't be as hard as you imagine.

INTRODUCTION

Learning a language is like learning a song. First you learn the melody, then the words, and then the many verses. You must practice out loud until the "melody" becomes familiar. The vocabulary (the words to the song) must be committed to memory. Most of the vocabulary used in this book are words you will use often in the classroom, so you will get plenty of practice.

You will start with the basics of pronunciation. Practice out loud so you get used to the sounds of the language. Then go on to the elementary grammar points, useful verbs, and then the vocabulary and activities you will need for classroom use.

Practice exercises are provided after each grammar point so you can check how you are progressing. The answers are provided in Appendix A. If you make mistakes, go back and review the explanation concerning that point.

Above all, don't be afraid of making a mistake. You will get better with time and practice. Take advantage of any Spanish-speaking students in your class. They will be happy to "teach the teacher," and their classmates will be impressed with their special talent.

Chapter One
Basics of Pronunciation

This chapter will discuss:
- ♦ Pronunciation
- ♦ Accents and Stress
- ♦ Practice Reading

PRONUNCIATION

Every language has unique sounds and rhythms. In order to get your ear accustomed to these sounds and rhythms, you will need to listen and practice. Listening to language tapes and music tapes with clear vocalists are good ways to do this. At this point, however, don't try to understand what is being said or sung. Listen to the sounds. Do this while relaxing. Let the sounds sink in and become a part of your subconscious.

Let's begin with the basic sounds of the language. How is it pronounced? Where does the stress go? What makes Spanish different?

EL ALFABETO EN ESPAÑOL—The Spanish Alphabet

A	*ah*	J	*jota*	R	*ere*
B	*be*	K	*ka*	rr	*erre*
C	*ce*	L	*ele*	S	*ese*
Ch	*che*	Ll	*elle*	T	*te*
D	*de*	M	*eme*	U	*u*
E	*e*	N	*ene*	V	*ve*
F	*efe*	Ñ	*eñe*	W	*doble ve*
G	*ge*	O	*o*	X	*equis*
H	*hache*	P	*pe*	Y	*y griega*
I	*i*	Q	*cu*	Z	*zeta*

LAS VOCALES—The Vowels

1. Spanish vowels usually have only ONE sound each:

A	as in	"mama"
E	as in	"pet" (sometimes long A = "day")
I	as in	"eeek!"
O	as in	"oh!" (short and snappy)
U	as in	"boo!"

♦ *LET'S PRACTICE*
Practice saying these words out loud. Be sure the same vowels keep the same sound each time:

casa	rata	gata	amiga	banana
house	mouse	cat	friend	banana

nene	Pepe	este	Teresa	elefante
baby		this		elephant

isla	iris	tigre	sí	medicina
island	iris	tiger	yes	medicine

ocho	otro	pronto	oso	famoso
eight	other	soon	bear	famous

uno	uva	usted	unir	universidad
one	grape	you	unite	university

2. Vowel blends:

ai	*ay*	baile	dance
au	*ow*	auto	car
ei	*long a*	seis	six
ia	*yah*	media	half
ie	*yeh*	siete	seven
io	*yoh*	dios	god
ua	*wah*	cuatro	four
ue	*wey*	bueno	good

LOS CONSONANTES—The Consonants

1. Consonants:

b & v	a blend of both sounds, a softer "b" bota and vota sound the same	**bota** **vota** boot vote
c	hard before a/o/u	**casa** **cosa** **cubo** house thing cube
	soft before e/i	**cena** **cinco** dinner five
d	softer than English, more like "th"	**dónde** **dedo** where finger
g	hard before a/o/u	**gato** **gota** **gusto** cat drop taste
	soft before e/i	**gente** **gigante** ("h") people giant
h	is silent	
j	sounds like "h"	**julio** **ojo** July eye
ll	sounds like "y" in yellow	**llave** **amarillo** key yellow
ñ	sounds like "ny" in canyon	**niño** boy
*rr	is trilled, a purring sound	**perro** dog
x	sometimes sounds like "h"	**México**
	sometimes sounds like "eks"	**extra**
y	like English "y" when beginning a word	**yo** I
	like "ee" when used alone	**y** and
z	sounds like "s"	**feliz** **zapato** happy shoe

---

* Don't worry if you can't trill the "rr." You will still be understood.

2. Note:

"gue"	sounds like "gue" as in "guest"	**guerra** war
"gui"	sounds like "gee" as in "geese"	**guía** guide
"qui"	sounds like "key" never "kwee"	**quién** who
"que"	sounds like "kay" never "kway"	**porque** because

exceptions: **pingüino**   "pin-GWEE-no"   penguin
                bilingüe   "bee-LIN-gway"   bilingual

♦ *LET'S PRACTICE*
Say the following out loud:

Me gusta el perro.
I like the dog.

Me llamo José.
My name is Joe.

Quiero bailar.
I want to dance.

hombre y mujer
man and woman

¿Quién habla?
Who is speaking?

¿Cuánto cuesta?
How much does it cost?

¿Por qué?
Why?

Tiene ojos azules.
He has blue eyes.

cinco niños
five children

once caballos
eleven horses

ACCENTS AND STRESS

1. If a word ends in a vowel, N, or S, the stress naturally falls on the second to the last syllable:

    e-le-FAN-te   GA-to   es-CUE-la   do-MIN-go

2. If it doesn't end in a vowel, N, or S, the stress will land on the last syllable:

    ciu-DAD   pa-PEL   fe-LIZ   ha-BLAR   co-MER   vi-VIR

3. Exceptions to these rules call for an accent to show the stressed syllable:

    le-ÓN   te-LÉ-fo-no   SÁ-ba-do   JÓ-ven-es
    Think of these accents as saying: "HIT ME HERE!"

4. Accents are also used to distinguish between words that are spelled alike and sound alike but have different meanings:

el	the	**él**	he	**si**	if	**sí**	yes
tu	your	**tú**	you	**mi**	my	**mí**	to me

5. All question and exclamation words carry an accent:

quién	**qué**	**dónde**	**cuándo**	**cómo**	**cuánto**	**cuál**
who	what	where	when	how	how many	which

¿Quién habla?	**¿Qué tal?**	**¿Dónde está?**
Who is speaking?	What's new?	Where is it?

¡Qué lástima!	**¡Qué bien!**	**¡Qué estúpido!**
What a pity!	How nice!	How stupid!

6. Accents are also used in verb conjugations. They can change both the tense and the subject:

hablo I speak   **habló** he spoke

7. Capital letters in Spanish do not show the accent marks:

águila, Aguila   **sábado SABADO**   **miércoles, MIERCOLES**

This does not change how the word is pronounced. Just remember that without the captials, the accents are still at work.

PRACTICE READING

(Remember: "H" is silent and "J", "X", and "ge" say /h/)

¡Hola! Me llamo Señora Jiménez.	Hello! My name is Mrs. Jiménez.
Trabajo como maestra	I work as a teacher
en la escuela primaria, San Xavier.	in the elementary school, San Xavier.
Enseño el tercer grado.	I teach the third grade.
En mi clase aprendemos	In my class we learn
la lectura, la matemática,	reading, math,
la escritura, la ciencia,	writing, science,
el arte, la historia,	art, history,
la geografía, la música,	geography, music,
el español, y la educación física.	Spanish, and physical education.
Tengo veinte y cinco estudiantes	I have twenty-five students
en mi clase.	in my class.

POINTS TO REMEMBER

1. When using the numbers **uno, primero,** and **tercero,** the "o" is dropped before a singular masculine noun:

    un estudiante   **el primer día**   **el tercer grado**
    one student   the first day   the third grade

    Here are more ordinal numbers:

primero	1st	**sexto**	6th
segundo	2nd	**séptimo**	7th
tercero	3rd	**octavo**	8th
cuarto	4th	**noveno**	9th
quinto	5th	**décimo**	10th

2. Notice that the definite article (**el** or **la**) is used with school studies: **la historia, el arte,** etc.

3. Notice that **español** (Spanish) is not capitalized. Neither are days of the week or months of the year. Only countries and proper names are capitalized.

4. Now do the practice reading again but substitute your own name, school, grade, etc.

Chapter Two

Agreement, Plurals, Adjectives, Questions, Possession, and Other Grammar Tips

This chapter will discuss:

- ♦ Agreement: Gender and Number
- ♦ Adjectives
- ♦ Making Plurals
- ♦ Making Questions
- ♦ Possession

AGREEMENT OF GENDER AND NUMBER

GENDER

1. Nouns in Spanish have gender: masculine or feminine. Gender is indicated by the definite and indefinite articles preceding the nouns:

masculine	feminine	
el, los	**la, las**	the
un, unos	**una, unas**	a, some

It's important to learn the articles with the nouns. The gender of nouns has no relation to males and females unless referring to persons or animals:

el maestro	the male teacher
la maestra	the female teacher
un perro	a male dog
una perra	a female dog

7

2. *Usually* you can tell the gender of a noun by its ending. Nouns ending in -o are masculine, those ending in -a are feminine.

    la escuela   **el libro**   **una silla**   **un escritorio**
    the school   the book   a chair   a desk

3. But what about nouns that end in some other letter? Aha! Those you must memorize. Examples:

    el papel   **el lápiz**   **el color**   **la clase**   **la mujer**
    the paper   the pencil   the color   the class   the woman

4. Then there are some "stinkers" that defy the rules:

    la mano   the hand   **el problema**   the problem
    el mapa   the map   **el día**   the day

    (Crazy, huh? Just remember: the noun endings will tell the gender most of the time. The rest you memorize.)

    ♦ *LET'S PRACTICE*
    Write **el** or **la** with each noun

    _____ **ventana**   _____ **puerta**   _____ **gato**   _____ **lápiz**

    _____ **maestro**   _____ **oficina**   _____ **clase**   _____ **mano** (!)

    _____ **zapato**   _____ **mapa** (!)   _____ **número**   _____ **mujer**

NUMBER

1. Nouns and adjectives must agree in number, too.

    The definite articles **el** and **la** become **los** and **las**
    The indefinite articles **un** and **una** become **unos** and **unas**
    Notice the plural endings all across in Spanish:

    Las **casas rojas son grandes**.
    The red houses are big.

    Los **estudiantes son inteligentes**.
    The students are intelligent.

    Unas **sillas están sucias**.
    Some chairs are dirty.

2. Number is also reflected in questions:

    ¿Cuántos días en una semana?
    How many days in a week?

    ¿Cuáles son las cuatro estaciones?
    What are the four seasons?

¿Cuántas pelotas tenemos?
How many balls do we have?

◆ *LET'S PRACTICE*
Make these into plurals:

el gato blanco _____

la clase grande _____

un niño inteligente _____

una muchacha alta _____

¿Cuál libro? _____

ADJECTIVES

PLACEMENT OF ADJECTIVES

1. In Spanish the adjective usually *follows* the noun.

el autobús amarillo	the yellow bus
la silla pequeña	the small chair
unos libros grandes	some big books
unas muchachas inteligentes	some intelligent girls

2. Sometimes the adjective will precede the noun. This is done for emphasis or to change the meaning.

un hombre pobre	a poor man (no money)
un pobre hombre	a poor man (pitiful)

OPPOSITES

grande*	**pequeño**	big	little
bonito	**feo**	pretty	ugly
gordo	**delgado**	fat	thin
bueno	**malo**	good	bad
viejo	**joven**	old	young
alto	**bajo**	tall	short
limpio	**sucio**	clean	dirty
abierto	**cerrado**	open	closed

caliente*	**frío**	hot	cold
nuevo	**viejo**	new	old
rico	**pobre***	rich	poor
feliz*	**triste***	happy	sad
mucho	**poco**	many	few
rápido	**despacio**	fast	slow
largo	**corto**	long	short
claro	**oscuro**	light	dark
derecha	**izquierda**	right	left
fácil*	**difícil***	easy	hard
verdad*	**mentira***	true	false
primero	**último**	first	last

*These adjectives will stay the same for masculine and feminine. They *will change* for plurals.

MORE ADJECTIVES

listo	ready
perezoso	lazy
cada*	every
todo	all
simpático	nice
importante*	important
inteligente*	intelligent
interesante*	interesting
excelente*	excellent

*No change for gender agreement

♦ *LET'S PRACTICE*
Show agreement in number and gender.

Examples:
new school = **escuela nueva**
dirty shoes = **zapatos sucios**

open book _____

small children _____

new papers _____

big class _____

hot day _____

old shoes _____

nice teacher _____

interesting stories _____

¡MUY BIEN!

MAKING PLURALS

In English we make plurals by adding -s or -es. The same is true in Spanish.

1. For words that end in a vowel, add -s

la casa	**las casas**	house
la tiza	**las tizas**	chalk
el padre	**los padres**	father
el coquí	**los coquís**	frog (a Puerto Rican frog)
el libro	**los libros**	book
la tribu	**las tribus**	tribe
el hombre	**los hombres**	man

2. For words that end in consonants, add -es

el árbol	**los árboles**	tree
el león	**los leones**	lion
la ciudad	**las ciudades**	city
el reloj	**los relojes**	clock
la flor	**las flores**	flower
el mes	**los meses**	month
la mujer	**las mujeres**	woman
el joven	**los jóvenes**	youth

3. This rule also applies to adjectives that agree with their nouns in number:

azul	**azules**	blue
gris	**grises**	gray
igual	**iguales**	equal
par	**pares**	even

4.   Sometimes adding a syllable, such as -es, will cause an accent to disappear:

león	**leones**	**lección**	**lecciones**
lion	lions	lesson	lessons

And sometimes the accent is stubborn and stays put!

fácil	**fácilmente**	**árbol**	**árboles**
easy	easily	tree	trees

5.   With words that end in -z in the singular, the -z becomes -c in the plural:

lápiz	**lápices**	**feliz**	**felices**
pencil	pencils	happy	happy

nariz	**narices**	**voz**	**voces**
nose	noses	voice	voices

♦ LET'S PRACTICE
Practice making plural nouns and adjectives:

niño _____   **silla** _____
boy   chair

olor _____   **papel** _____
smell   paper

tren _____   **pez** _____
train   fish

clase _____   **luz** _____
class   light

día _____   **noche** _____
day   night

maestra _____   **pelota** _____
teacher   ball

hermano _____   **verde** _____
brother   green

joven _____   **canción** _____
youth   song

bandera_____   **azul** _____
flag   blue

flor _____   **árbol** _____
flower   tree

lápiz _____   **feliz** _____
pencil   happy

MAKING QUESTIONS

1. Questions in Spanish usually start with the verb:

    ¿Habla usted español?   **¿Tiene usted un lápiz?**
    Do you speak Spanish?   Do you have a pencil?

2. The subject can be omitted when it is understood in the verb ending:

    ¿Vives en Arizona?   **¿Estamos listos?**
    Do you live in Arizona?   Are we ready?

3. A regular sentence can be turned into a question by raising the inflection at the end:

    ¿Juan tiene la pelota?
    John has the ball?

4. All written questions are introduced by ¿ and concluded with?

5. Basic question words:

    ¿Quién? **¿Qué?**   **¿Dónde?**   **¿Cuándo?**   **¿Cómo?**   **¿Cuánto?**   **¿Cuál?**
    who   what   where   when   how   how much   which

USEFUL QUESTIONS

¿Cómo te llamas?	What's your name? (How do you call yourself?)
¿Hablas inglés?	Do you speak English?
¿Cuántos años tienes?	How old are you? (How many years do you have?)
¿Dónde vives?	Where do you live?
¿Quién es tu maestra?	Who is your teacher?
¿Qué es esto?	What is this?
¿Cuándo comemos?	When do we eat?

POSSESSION

There is no "apostrophe s" in Spanish.

1. Possession can be shown by using "de." Example:

¿De quién es este libro?	Whose book is this?
Es *de* Tara.	It's Tara's.
Es el libro *de* Tara.	It is Tara's book.
El libro *de* Bob es rojo.	Bob's book is red.

(And then there's "del"!)

El libro *del* niño es azul.	The boy's book is blue.

2. Possession can be shown using possessive adjectives. They must agree in number with the noun modified. "Ours" must also agree in gender with the noun.

mi, mis	my	**nuestro, nuestros**	our
tu, tus	your	**nuestra, nuestras**	our
su, sus	your, his	**su, sus**	your
su, sus	hers, its	**su, sus**	their

Examples:

mi camisa	**mis zapatos**
my shirt	my shoes
tu amigo	**tus amigos**
your friend	your friends
su hermano	**sus hermanos**
his brother	his brothers
	also: her, your, their brother/s
nuestra casa	**nuestros niños**
our house	our children

OTHER POINTS TO REMEMBER

1. AL and DEL

When "a" (to) and "de" (of) are in front of "el" (the), they become "al" and "del."

a + el = al   de + el = del

This never happens with "la," "los," or "las."

example:

	Voy _al_ mercado.	I'm going _to the_ market.
(but)	**Voy _a la_ escuela.**	I'm going _to the_ school.

	La luz _del_ sol	the light _of the_ sun
(but)	**La luz _de la_ luna**	the light _of the_ moon

2. HAY

In the present tense use "hay" (pronounced "ay") or "no hay" for "there is, there are, there isn't, there aren't."

Hay **cinco muchachas en la clase.**
There are five girls in the class.

Hay **una maestra. Hay un maestro.**
There is one teacher.

No hay **perros en la clase.**
There are no dogs in the class.

¿Cuántos estudiantes _hay_ en esta clase?
How many students _are there_ in this class?

¿_Hay_ una fiesta hoy?
Is there a party today?

♦ _LET'S PRACTICE_
Use "al" or "del" where appropriate:

1. **Es la mesa de (el estudiante).** _____

2. **Es el lápiz de (la maestra).** _____

3. **Me gustan los cuentos de (los niños).** _____

4. **Voy a (la oficina).** _____

5. **Voy a (el parque).** _____

6. **Me gusta enseñar a (los niños).** _____

Show possession:

¿De quién es este suéter?   **Es de Tara.**
Whose sweater is this?   It's Tara's.

7. It's Robbyn's. _____

8. It's Jackson's. _____

9. It's the teacher's. (feminine) _____

10. It's the teacher's. (masculine) _____

11. It's the boy's. _____

12. my pencil _____

13. our school _____

14. her friends _____

15. your chair (use familiar, singular form) _____

¿Cómo se dice en español?
How do you say this in Spanish?

1. There are thirty students in my class. _____

2. Is there a teacher? _____

3. There isn't (any) chalk. **(tiza)** _____

4. How many books are there? _____

5. How many days are there in a week? _____

¿

¡EXCELENTE!

Chapter Three
Verbs to Know, Basic Present Tense

This chapter will discuss:

- ♦ Verbs to Know: Tener   Llamarse
  -                              Ser   Gustar
  -                              Estar   Ir

- ♦ Present Tense: -AR, -ER, -IR Verbs

VERBS TO KNOW

Here are a few verbs that will be useful in everyday situations. Memorize them! Subject pronouns are not always used before verbs in Spanish because the verb ending indicates who is speaking. However, since the same verb endings are used for **usted, él, ella** and **ustedes, ellos, ellas,** use the subject pronouns with the verb to be clear.

Subject pronouns:

yo	I	**nosotros**	we
tú	you (familiar)		
usted	you (formal)	**ustedes**	you (formal)
él	he	**ellos**	they
ella	she	**ellas**	they (fem)

Note: There is no subject pronoun in Spanish for "it."

Use the "he/she" singular form.

(el cuento)	**Es interesante.**	**(la fiesta)**	**Es para la clase.**
(the story)	It is interesting.	(the party)	It's for the class.

17

TU VERSUS USTED

Spanish has two forms of "you" singular: **tú** and **usted**.

Use **tú** with children and close friends.

Use **usted** when showing respect.

Children *always* use **usted** with parents and teachers.

They use **tú** with each other.

Think of when you call someone by a first name or use their title. The same rules govern **tú** and **usted**.

There is a plural form of **tú** but it is not used in the U.S. or Mexico in general speech.

Use **ustedes** in both formal and informal situations.

VERBS

TENER—to have

yo	tengo	nosotros	tenemos
tú	tienes		
usted	tiene	ustedes	tienen
él	tiene	ellos	tienen
ella	tiene	ellas	tienen

TENER has lots of uses:

to have:	**Yo tengo un gato**.	I have a cat.
telling age:	**Tengo seis años**.	I am six years old.
being correct:	**Tienes razón**.	You're right.
conditions:	**¿Qué tienes?**	What's the matter?
	Tengo frío.	I'm cold.
	Tengo calor.	I'm hot.
	Tengo hambre.	I'm hungry.
	Tengo sed.	I'm thirsty.
	Tengo miedo.	I'm scared.
	Tengo sueño.	I'm sleepy.
	Tengo prisa.	I'm in a hurry.
	Tengo dolor.	I hurt.

SER AND ESTAR—to be

Spanish has two "to be" verbs: SER and ESTAR. One is for permanent conditions of being, the other for changeable conditions of being.

SER—to be (permanent)

yo	soy	nosotros	somos
tú	eres		
usted	es	ustedes	son
él	es	ellos	son
ella	es	ellas	son

1. **Soy maestra.**   (profession, identification)
   I'm a teacher.

2. **Eres bonito.**   (inherent characteristic)
   You're pretty.

3. **El es simpático.**   (inherent characteristic)
   He's nice.

4. **Es de María.**   (showing possession)
   It's Maria's.

5. **Es de papel.**   (what it's made of)
   It's made of paper.

6. **Somos americanos.**   (nationality)
   We're Americans.

7. **Son de México.**   (place of origin)
   They are from Mexico.

8. **Son las dos.**   (telling time)*
   It's two o'clock.

---

*Yes, it's true, time will change. But all the same, always use "ser" when telling time.

ESTAR—to be (temporary)

yo	estoy	nosotros	estamos
tú	estás		
usted	está	ustedes	están
él	está	ellos	están
ella	está	ellas	están

1. **Estoy triste.**   (changeable condition)
   I'm sad.

2. **Estás sucio.**   (changeable description)
   You're dirty.

3. **Está enfermo.**   (health)
   She's sick.

4. **Estamos en Arizona.**   (location)
   We are in Arizona.

5. **Están en la clase.**   (location! location! location!)
   They are in the class.

LLAMARSE—to call yourself

"Llamarse" is a reflexive verb. You must use the reflexive pronouns "me," "te," "se," and "nos" for "myself," "yourself," "himself," etc.

> **Me llamo**—I call myself   **Nos llamamos**—We call ourselves

You can also say "**Mi nombre es....**" which more closely matches "My name is...." However, DO NOT mix them up and say "Mi llamo es...."

It's either: "**Me llamo....**" or "**Mi nombre es...**"

Me llamo	**Nos llamamos**
Te llamas	
Se llama	**Se llaman**

1. **¿Cómo te llamas?**
   What is your name?
   Me llamo ....
   My name is........

2. **¿Cómo se llama su maestra?**
   What is your teacher's name?
   Se llama ....
   Her/His name is ....

3. **¿Cómo se llaman tus padres?**
   What are your parents' names?
   Se llaman Jorge y Adela Johnson.
   Their names are George and Adela Johnson

4. **¿Cómo se llama tu escuela?**
   What is your school's name?
   Se llama "Quail Run Elementary."
   It's called "Quail Run Elementary."

GUSTAR—to like

¡ME GUSTA HABLAR ESPAÑOL!

To say you like something in Spanish is quite different than in English. In Spanish we don't do the liking. Something is "pleasing to us." You must pay attention to what is doing the pleasing. Is it singular or plural?

In English we say: I like tacos.
In Spanish we say: **Me gustan los tacos.**
Tacos are pleasing to me.

The good news is, you have only two forms of the verb to learn in the present tense: gusta, gustan. Either one thing or a plural of things is pleasing you.

The "bad" news is, you must learn the indirect object pronoun that fits who is talking:

me	to me
te	to you
le	to you, to him, to her
nos	to us
les	to you, to them

Me gusta, me gustan	**Nos gusta, nos gustan**
Te gusta, te gustan	
Le gusta, le gustan	**Les gusta, les gustan**

1.	**Me gusta la sopa.**	I like the soup.
2.	**No nos gusta la sopa.**	We don't like the soup.
3.	**Nos gustan los tacos.**	We like tacos.
4.	**No me gustan los tacos.**	I don't like tacos.
5.	**¿Te gusta el color rojo?**	Do you like the color red?
6.	**Sí, me gusta el color rojo.**	Yes, I like the color red.
7.	**¿Les gustan los perros?**	Do you (plural) like dogs?
8.	**Sí, nos gustan los perros.**	Yes, we like dogs.
9.	**¿Le gusta estudiar?***	Does he like to study?
10.	**Sí, le gusta estudiar.**	Yes, he likes to study.

---

*When using a verb in the infinitive, use the singular form of GUSTAR: **Me gusta hablar español.**
I like to speak Spanish.
Nos gusta bailar.
We like to dance.

NEVER say: Me gusto... Remember: You don't do the liking.

IR—to go

yo	voy	nosotros	vamos
tú	vas		
usted	va	ustedes	van
él	va	ellos	van
ella	va	ellas	van

Yo voy a México.	I am going to Mexico.
Tú vas a casa.	You are going home.
Ella va a la oficina.	She is going to the office.
Vamos a jugar.	We are going to play.*
Ellos van a la escuela.	They go to school.

---

*Use "IR" to talk in the future. You don't need to learn a future tense yet. Use this formula: IR + a + infinitive

1. **Esta tarde *voy a leer* un cuento.**
   This afternoon I'm going to read a story.

2. **Joe *va a hacer* el calendario la semana que viene.**
   Joe will do the calendar next week.

3. **Los niños *van a visitar* el museo mañana.**
   The children will visit the museum tomorrow.

You can also use the following formula to say, "Let's do something."

Vamos a + infinitive of verb

Vamos a leer.	Let's read.
Vamos a cantar.	Let's sing.
Vamos a jugar.	Let's play.
Vamos a salir.	Let's go out.
Vamos a formar una línea.	Let's get in line.
Vamos a mirar el video.	Let's watch the video.
Vamos a aprender español.	Let's learn Spanish.
Vamos a hablar español.	Let's speak Spanish.
Vamos a escuchar.	Let's listen.
Vamos a comer.	Let's eat.
Vamos a escribir.	Let's write.
Vamos a sentarnos.	Let's sit down.
Vamos a levantarnos.	Let's stand up.
Vamos a callarnos.	Let's get quiet.

♦ *LET'S PRACTICE*
Practice using the verb TENER:

1. _____ un libro.   (I have a book.)

2. _____ mi lápiz.   (You have my pencil.)

3. _____ ocho años.   (He is eight years old.)

4. _____ hambre.   (We're hungry.)

5. Mis gatos _____ miedo.   (My cats are scared.)

♦ *LET'S PRACTICE*
Practice using the verb SER:

6. _____ la maestra.   (I am the teacher.)

7. _____ de Guatemala.   (We are from Guatemala.)

8. Juan _____ mi amigo.   (Juan is my friend.)

9. María _____ mexicana.   (María is Mexican.)

10. La casa _____ de adobe.   (The house is made of adobe.)

♦ *LET'S PRACTICE*
Practice using the verb ESTAR: (temporary conditions)

11. ¿ _____ triste?   (Are you sad?)

12. _____ enfermo.   (I am sick.)

13. ¿Dónde _____ José?   (Where is José?)

14. _____ en la oficina.   (He is in the office.)

15. Los niños _____ sucios.   (The children are dirty.)

♦ *LET'S PRACTICE*
Practice using the verb LLAMARSE:

(This is a reflexive verb so you must use the reflexive pronouns that match the subject: **me, te, se, nos, se.**)

1. ¿Cómo _____?   (What's your name?)

2. _____ Rita.   (My name is Rita.)

3. Mi escuela _____ Adams.   (My school is called Adams.)

4. _____"Los Tigres."   (We call ourselves "The Tigers.")

5. ¿Cómo _____ tus padres?   (What are your parents called?)

♦ *LET'S PRACTICE*
Practice using the verb GUSTAR:

(Remember: You don't do the liking. Something pleases you.)

6. _____ el color rojo.   (I like the color red.)

7. ¿ _____ los gatos?   (Do you like cats?) (Use **tú**)

8. No _____ bailar.   (He doesn't like to dance.)

9. _____ estudiar.   (We like to study.)

10. _____ los sábados.   (I like Saturdays.)

♦ *LET'S PRACTICE*
Practice using the verb IR:

11. _____ a la oficina.   (I'm going to the office.)

12. _____ a cantar.   (Let's sing.)

13. Mateo _____ a la escuela.   (Mateo goes to school.)

14. ¿ _____ a la fiesta?   (Are you going to the party?)

15. Ellos no _____ conmigo.   (They aren't going with me.)

How did you do? Check your answers with those in Appendix A.

VERB CONJUGATION—PRESENT TENSE

The infinitive of Spanish verbs is shown by the suffixes -ar, -er, -ir. For example: **hablar** means to speak. To conjugate a verb, the infinitive ending is dropped and subject endings are added: **habl + o = hablo** (I speak).

Many verbs in Spanish are irregular and do not follow these basic rules for conjugation. Some of the more common irregular verbs are listed on the previous pages.

The good news is, the -ar ending is the **most common** of all Spanish verbs. So once you master these endings, you are well on your way to conjugating lots of Spanish verbs.

-AR VERBS

(yo)	-o	(nosotros)	-amos
(tú)	-as		
(usted)	-a	(ustedes)	-an
(él, ella)	-a	(ellos, ellas)	-an

Hablar—to speak
(*habl + endings*)

yo hablo	nosotros hablamos
tú hablas	
usted habla	ustedes hablan
él, ella habla	ellos, ellas hablan

-ER, -IR VERBS

These two sets of endings are almost the same. A change is made only in the "we" form.

(yo) -o	**(nosotros) -emos, imos**
(tú) -es	
(usted) -e	**(ustedes) -en**
(él, ella) -e	**(ellos, ellas) -en**

Aprender—to learn
(*aprend + endings*)

yo aprendo	nosotros aprendemos
tú aprendes	
usted aprende	ustedes aprenden
él, ella aprende	ellos, ellas aprenden

Vivir—to live
(*viv + endings*)

yo vivo	nosotros vivimos
tú vives	
usted vive	ustedes viven
él, ella vive	ellos, ellas viven

Note: Remember, we are skipping the plural "tú" form.

♦ LET'S PRACTICE

Conjugate the following -ar verbs. Remember, just drop the -ar suffix and tack on the subject endings. Example:

trabajar (to work)   **trabajo, trabajas, trabaja, trabajamos, trabajan**

1. **estudiar**   (to study)
2. **caminar**   (to walk)
3. **cantar**   (to sing)

Now try these -er verbs:

4. **comer**   (to eat)
5. **leer**   (to read)
6. **correr**   (to run)

Now try these -ir verbs:

7. **escribir**   (to write)
8. **decidir**   (to decide)

Una adivinanza:	*A Riddle:*
Yo tengo una tía,	I have an aunt,
Mi tía tiene una hermana,	My aunt has a sister,
Y la hermana de mi tía	And the sister of my aunt
No es mi tía.	Is not my aunt.
¿Quién es?	Who is it?
(mi madre)	(my mother)

GETTING GOOD AT THIS, AREN'T YOU?

Chapter Four

Classroom Spanish, Pledge of Allegiance, Daily Usage

This chapter will discuss:
- ♦ Classroom Spanish
- ♦ Calendar
- ♦ Weather
- ♦ Parts of the Body

CLASSROOM SPANISH

¡Hola!	Hi!
Buenos días.	Good morning.
Buenas tardes.	Good afternoon.
Me llamo	My name is .....
¿Cómo te llamas?	What's your name?
¿Cómo están?	How are you? (plural)
Voy a pasar la lista.	I'm going to call the roll.
Presente	Here (answering roll call)
¿Cuántos niños hay?	How many children are there?
¿Quién no está?	Who isn't here?
¿Qué día es hoy?	What is the day today?
Gracias	Thank you
De nada	You're welcome
Por favor	Please
Perdón	Pardon
¡Siéntate! / ¡Siéntense!	Sit down! (singular/plural)
¡Levántate! / ¡Levántense!	Stand up! (singular/plural)
Levanta la mano.	Raise your hand.

Baja la mano.	Put your hand down.
Abran sus libros.	Open your books.
Cierren sus libros.	Close your books.
Escucha / Escuchen	Listen (singular/plural)
Repite / Repitan	Repeat (singular/plural)
Mira / Miren	Look (singular/plural)
Otra vez	Again
Todos juntos	All together
¡Silencio!	Quiet!
¡Muy bien!	Very good!
Vamos a leer un cuento.	Let's read a story.
¿Listo? ¿Listos?	Ready
¿Cómo se dice en español?	How do you say it in Spanish?
¿Quién tiene.....?	Who has........?
¿Dónde está......?	Where is.......?
¿Dónde están.....?	Where are......?
¿Qué es esto?	What's this?
Dame (Denme) _____	Give me _____ (singular/plural)
Adiós	Goodbye
Hasta la vista	See you later
Hasta mañana	Until tomorrow
Hasta lunes	Until Monday
Nos vemos mañana.	We'll see each other tomorrow.

DAILY DIALOGUE

Teacher:	**Buenos días, clase.** Good morning, class.
Class:	**Buenos días, Señora/Señorita/Señor—** Good morning, Mrs./Miss/Mr.—
Teacher:	**¿Cómo están ustedes?** How are you?
Class:	**Muy bien, gracias. ¿Y usted?** Very well, thanks. And you?
Teacher:	**Muy bien, gracias.** Very well, thanks.

Other Responses

Así, así	**No muy bien**	**Lo siento mucho.**
So-so	Not very well	I'm very sorry.

EL JURAMENTO A LA BANDERA—The Pledge of Allegiance

Juro lealtad
a la bandera
de los Estados Unidos de América,
y a la república
que representa
una nación
bajo Dios
indivisible
con libertad y justicia para todos.

EL CALENDARIO—THE CALENDAR

Days, months, and seasons are not capitalized in Spanish.

LOS DIAS DE LA SEMANA—Days of the Week

lunes	Monday (always begin on Monday)
martes	Tuesday
miércoles	Wednesday
jueves	Thursday
viernes	Friday
sábado	Saturday
domingo	Sunday

LOS MESES DEL AÑO—Months of the Year

enero	January	**abril**	April
febrero	February	**mayo**	May
marzo	March	**junio**	June

julio	July	**octubre**	October
agosto	August	**noviembre**	November
septiembre	September	**diciembre**	December

LAS ESTACIONES DEL AÑO—Seasons

la primavera	**el verano**	**el otoño**	**el invierno**
Spring	Summer	Fall	Winter

THE MORNING ROUTINE

Maestra: **Buenos días, clase. ¿Qué día es hoy?**
Good morning, class. What day is today?

Clase: **Hoy es lunes.**
Today is Monday.

Maestra: **¿Qué día fue ayer?**
What day was yesterday?

Clase: **Ayer fue domingo.**
Yesterday was Sunday.

Maestra: **¿Qué día es mañana?**
What day is tomorrow?

Clase: **Mañana es martes.**
Tomorrow is Tuesday.

Maestra: **¿Cuáles son los días de la semana?**
What are the days of the week?

Clase: **Lunes, martes, miércoles, jueves, viernes, sábado y domingo.**
Monday, Tuesday, Wednesday, Thursday, Friday, Saturday, and Sunday.

Maestra: **¿En qué mes estamos?**
In what month are we?

Clase: **Noviembre.**
November.

Maestra: **¿Cuáles son los meses del año?**
What are the months of the year?

Clase: **Enero, febrero, marzo, abril, mayo, junio, julio, agosto, septiembre, octubre, noviembre, diciembre.**
January, February, March, April, May, June, July, August, September, October, November, December.

Maestra: **¿Cuáles son las estaciones del año?**
What are the seasons of the year?

Clase:	**La primavera, el verano, el otoño, el invierno.**
	Spring, summer, fall, winter.
Maestra:	**¿En qué estación estamos ahora?**
	In which season are we now?
Clase:	**El otoño.**
	Fall.
Maestra:	**¿Cuál es la fecha de hoy?**
	What is today's date?
Clase:	**Hoy es lunes, el diez de noviembre.**
	Today is Monday, the tenth of November.
Maestra:	**¿Y el año?**
	And the year?
Clase:	**Mil novecientos noventa y siete. (1997)**
	One thousand, nine hundred, ninety-seven
Maestra:	**¡Perfecto!**
	Perfect!

WEATHER

¿Qué tiempo hace?	What's the weather like?
Hace calor.	It's hot.
Hace frío.	It's cold.
Hace viento.	It's windy.
Está lloviendo.	It's raining.
Está nublado.	It's cloudy.
Está nevando.	It's snowing.
Hay neblina.	It's foggy.
Hace sol.	It's sunny.
Es un día soleado.	It's a sunny day.
el sol	sun
el cielo	sky
el viento	wind
la tormenta	storm
la lluvia	rain
la neblina	fog
el calor	heat

el frío	cold
la nieve	snow
las nubes	clouds
Hace buen tiempo.	It's good weather.
Hace mal tiempo.	It's bad weather.

PARTES DEL CUERPO—PARTS OF THE BODY

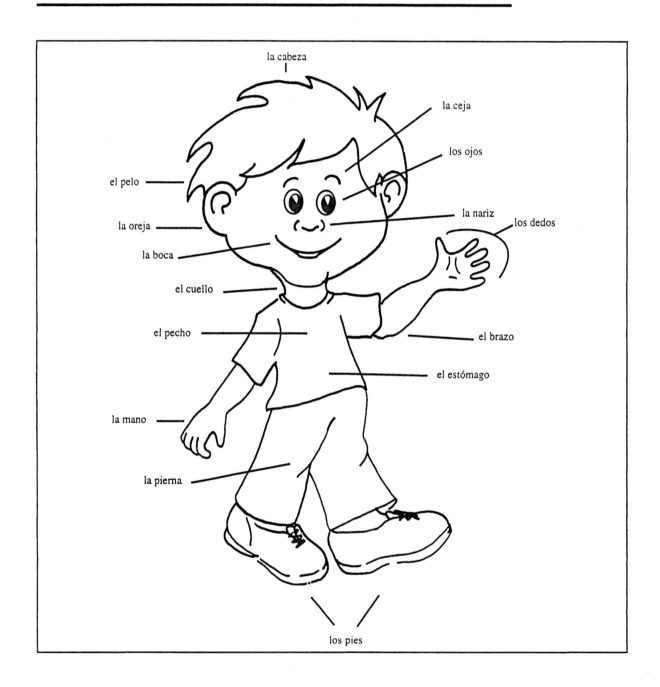

1. When talking about parts of the body in Spanish, use the definite article instead of a possessive.

2. There are two ways to talk about hurts:

using "duele(n)":	**Me duele el brazo.** My arm hurts.
	Le duele la cabeza. His head hurts.
using "tener":	**Tengo dolor del brazo.** I have an armache.
	Tiene dolor de la cabeza. He has a headache.

DIALOGO: DOLORES DEL CUERPO—Dialogue: Body Hurts

Maestra:	**¿Cómo estás, Marcos?** How are you, Marcos?
Marcos:	**No muy bien. Me duele la cabeza.** Not very well. My head hurts.
Maestra:	**Lo siento mucho. Vete a la enfermera.** I'm very sorry. Go to the nurse.
At the nurse's office:	
Marcos:	**No me siento bien.** I don't feel well.
Enfermera:	**¿Te duele el estómago?** Does your stomach hurt?
Marcos:	**No. Me duele la cabeza.** No. My head hurts.
Enfermera:	**Descansa un rato aquí.** Rest a while here.
Later:	
Enfermera:	**¿Todavía tienes dolor de cabeza?** Do you still have a headache?
Marcos:	**No. Ya no me duele la cabeza.** No. My head doesn't hurt anymore.
Enfermera:	**Muy bien. Puedes regresar a la clase.** Very good. You can return to class.

Marcos:

¡Ay! Ahora tengo dolor del brazo.
Oh! Now I have an armache.

Enfermera:

Dime, Marcos, ¿tienes un examen hoy?
Tell me, Marcos, do you have a test today?

Marcos:

Sí.
Yes.

Enfermera:

Ahora comprendo.
Now I understand.

Chapter Five

Math Vocabulary, Maya Math

This chapter will discuss:
- ◆ Math Vocabulary
- ◆ Telling Time
- ◆ Maya Math

LOS NUMEROS—THE NUMBERS

cero	catorce	veinte y ocho
uno	quince	veinte y nueve
dos	diez y seis	treinta (30)
tres	diez y siete	treinta y uno
cuatro	diez y ocho	treinta y dos
cinco	diez y nueve	treinta y cuatro
seis	veinte (20)	cuarenta (40)
siete	veinte y uno	cincuenta (50)
ocho	veinte y dos	sesenta (60)
nueve	veinte y tres	setenta (70)
diez (10)	veinte y cuatro	ochenta (80)
once	veinte y cinco	noventa (90)
doce	veinte y seis	cien....ciento uno, ciento dos,
trece	veinte y siete	dos cientos, tres cientos, etc.

MATH VOCABULARY

la matemática	math
los números	the numbers
contar	to count
más / y	plus, and
menos	minus, less
las unidades	the ones
las decenas	the tens
el problema	the problem (notice "el")
sumar	to add
restar	to subtract
dividir	to divide
multiplicar	to multiply
la fracción	the fraction
la mitad	the half
el cuarto	the quarter
tres cuartos	three quarters
la tercera parte	the third
¿Cuánto es?	How much is it?
¿Cuántos son?	How many are there?
¿Cuántas (manzanas) hay?	How many (apples) are there?
¿Cuántos (globos) hay?	How many (balloons) are there?
Vamos a contar a cien por diez.	Let's count to 100 by 10's.
Vamos a contar a veinte por cinco.	Let's count to 20 by 5's.

SUMAR Y RESTAR—Adding and Subtracting

¿Cuántos son dos más tres? — How much is two plus three?

$2 + 3 = 5$ **dos más tres son cinco**
dos y tres son cinco

¿Cuántos son siete más ocho? — How much is seven plus eight?

$7 + 8 = 15$ **siete más ocho son quince**

¿Cuántos son seis menos dos?　　　How much is six minus two?

6 - 2 = 4　　　**seis menos dos son cuatro**

¿Cuántos son diez menos nueve?

10 - 9 = 1　　　**diez menos nueve <u>es</u> uno**
　　　　　　　notice change from "son" to "es"
　　　　　　　one and zero are treated as singular nouns

5 - 5 = 0　　　**cinco menos cinco es cero**

OTHER

2 × 2 = 4　　　**dos por dos son cuatro**

10 ÷ 2 = 5　　　**diez dividido por dos son cinco**

♦ *LET'S PRACTICE*

¿Cómo se dice en español?

4 + 5 = 9	10 - 2 = 8	25 + 15 = 40
1 + 6 = 7	13 - 12 = 1	100 ÷ 20 = 5
0 + 1 = 1	16 - 11 = 5	3 × 3 = 9

NOTE: Your students will quickly learn to count in Spanish by rote. The real test comes when you flash a number at them and they must name it out of sequence.

TELLING TIME

Hours are feminine in Spanish: **la hora, las dos, las diez.** They are also usually plural, except time involving 1:00, noon, or midnight.

Asking the time, however, is always singular.

¿Qué hora es?　　　　　　What time is it?
　　2:00　　　　　　　　　　1:00
Son las dos.　　　　　　　**Es la una.**

How many minutes past the hour?　Use **y** (and).
　　3:20　　　　　　　　　　11:10
Son las tres y veinte.　　　**Son las once y diez.**

How many minutes to the hour?　Use **menos** (less).
　　2:45　　　　　　　　　　12:50
Son las tres menos quince.　**Es la una menos diez.**

Sometimes you will hear:

Faltan quince minutos para que sean las tres.

Fifteen minutes (lacking) for it to be three.

2:45

Is it half past?	Use **y media** (and half).
4:30	9:30
Son las cuatro y media.	**Son las nueve y media.**

Other time expressions:

Es la mañana.	It's morning.
Es la tarde.	It's afternoon.
Es la noche.	It's night.
Es el mediodía.	It's noon.
Es la medianoche.	It's midnight.
Es tarde.	It's late.
Es temprano.	It's early.
A las cinco de la mañana.	At five in the morning.
A las dos de la tarde.	At two in the afternoon.
A las ocho y media de la noche.	At eight-thirty at night.
Más vale tarde que nunca.	Better late than never!

<u>Una adivinanza:</u>	<u>A riddle:</u>
Ando y ando	I go and I go
Siempre estoy aquí	I am always here
Todos me miran la cara	Everyone looks at my face
No tengo ojos	I don't have eyes
No tengo nariz	I don't have a nose
No tengo boca	I don't have a mouth
Pero sí tengo manos	But I do have hands
¿Quién soy?	Who am I?

MAYA MATH

The Mayas of Mexico and Central America loved numbers! Their glyphs are full of them, noting dates of historical events. They used a system of dots, bars, and shells to write their numbers. Instead of base 10 that we use, they used base 20. Each dot equals 1 and each bar equals 5.

zero	1	2	3	4
5	6	7	8	9
10	11	12	13	14
15	16	17	18	19

Twenty was written like this, using the next level, or place value:

The Mayas developed the concepts of zero, represented by a shell, and place value. These concepts allowed them to write large numbers using rising levels. For example:

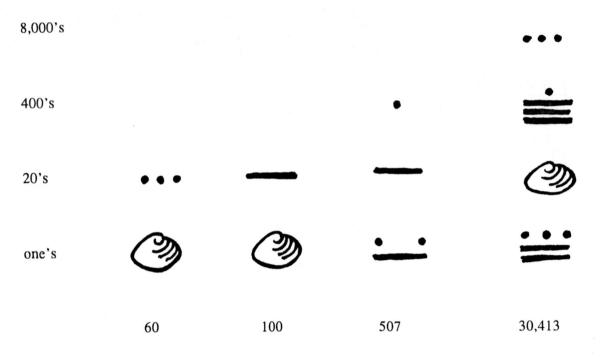

8,000's

400's

20's

one's

        60   100   507   30,413

Have students practice math the Maya way, with dots and bars. Let them recite the numbers they represent in Spanish.

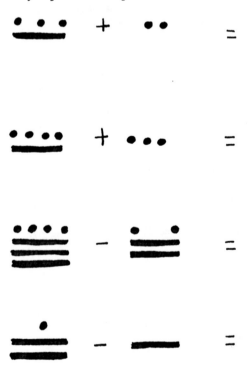

Chapter Six

Movement Activities, Games, Proverbs

This chapter will discuss:
- ♦ Movement Activities
- ♦ Games
- ♦ Proverbs

MOVEMENT ACTIVITIES

FLORES Y COLORES

Debajo de la tierra	squat with arms
Está una flor	folded across chest
Sube para arriba	rise, moving arms upward
Hacia el calor	palms together, overhead
Cae la lluvia	arms down half way like rain
Abre la flor	then open arms wide
Todos admiran	arms down at sides
Su lindo color:	and take a bow
¡Anaranjado, rojo, rosado	"flowers" jump up and down
Blanco, amarillo, azul y morado!	at end, give a loud clap

Translation: Under the earth is a flower. It rises up to the warmth. The rain falls down. The flower opens. Everyone admires its beautiful color. Orange, red, pink, white, yellow, blue and purple!

SHAPE MARCHING

Tape some music that sounds good for marching, jumping, running, or walking. As the music is played, students in the center of the room respond to commands:

"¡Marchen en un triángulo!"	March in a triangle!
"¡Brinquen en un cuadro!"	Jump in a square!
"¡Corran en un círculo!"	Run in a circle!
"¡Caminen en un rectángulo!"	Walk in a rectangle!
"¡Formen una línea a la puerta!"	Form a line at the door!

MANOS ARRIBA

	(standing)
Manos arriba	hands up
Da un salto	give a jump
Manos abajo	hands down
Da una vuelta	turn around
Un paso pa' adelante	one step forward
Un paso pa' atrás	one step back
Brinca, brinca	jump, jump
¡Ya no más!	no more! (shrug shoulders)
A la izquierda	to the left
Andarás	you'll walk
A la derecha	to the right
Volverás	you'll return
Un paso pa' adelante	one step forward
Un paso pa' atrás	one step back
Brinca, brinca	jump, jump
¡Ya no más!	no more! (shrug)

The translation is used only to show movement.

GAMES

SIMON DICE

This is a Spanish version of "Simon Says." It's a good way to practice vocabulary for parts of the body.

"Simón dice, ¡toca la cabeza!"   students touch their heads
"Simón dice, ¡toca la boca!"   students touch their mouths

BUT...

"¡Toca la mano!" calls for no action because there was no **"Simón dice"** at the start. The teacher can say:

"Simón no dijo, 'toca la mano'."
Simon didn't say....

LA LOTERIA

Spanish "Bingo" can be played with numbers, shapes, colors, or objects. Try to get the students to repeat the word called so they will learn new vocabulary, not just the picture. When "Bingo" or "Lotería" is called, ask the student to name the covered pictures or numbers in Spanish. As a math activity, use math bingo games, but call the numbers in Spanish. Make sure the students repeat the numbers in Spanish, too.

COLOR GAME

rojo	red	**amarillo**	yellow
azul	blue	**anaranjado**	orange
verde	green	**rosa/rosado**	pink
café	brown	**morado**	purple
gris	gray	**negro**	black
blanco	white		

Play this game after the students have learned the colors in Spanish. Pick a student and pin a strip of colored paper (green, for example) on his back, but don't let him see it. Turn the student around and show the class the color. The color-tagged student then begins to guess the color:

"¿Es rojo?"
"No es rojo," the class responds.

"¿Es blanco?"
"No es blanco."

The student keeps guessing colors until the correct color is guessed. Then the class says:

"**¡Sí, es verde!**"

A new player is then chosen. The children really like this game and will not want to stop playing!

¿QUIEN DICE?

Your students will need to learn animal names and animal sounds in Spanish to play this game. Youngsters are always surprised to learn that animals speak Spanish, too!

Divide the class into four teams. The teacher asks who makes certain animal sounds. If the teacher asks, "**¿Quién dice 'Ki-ki-ri-kí'?**" (Who says "Cock-a-doodle-do?) they must answer together, "**el gallo**" (the rooster). If they miss, the next team tries. If that team can give the answer, they get a point. The next "**¿Quién dice?**" goes to the next team, and so on.

A variation of this game is to ask teams to give the sounds the animals make:

Teacher: "**¿Qué dice el gallo?**"
               What does the rooster say?

Answer: "**Ki-ki-ri-kí**"

              ¿Qué dicen los animales?
              What do the animals say?

el gallo (the rooster)	**ki-ki-ri-kí**
la gallina (the hen)	**ca-ra-ca-ra** (or) **cla-cla-cla**
los pollitos (the chicks)	**pío-pío-pí**
el pato (the duck)	**cua-cua-cua**
el perro (the dog)	**guau-guau-guau**
el gato (the cat)	**miau-miau-miau**
el caballo (the horse)	**ji-ji-ji-ji-ji**
la oveja (the sheep)	**maaa-maaaa**
la vaca (the cow)	**muuu-muuuu**
la paloma (the dove)	**cu-cu-ca-ru**
la rana (the frog)	**glu-glu-glu**
el coquí (the Puerto Rican frog)	**coquí-coquí**
el burro (the donkey)	**ji-ja ji-ja**
el tecolote (the owl)	**uu-uu-uu-uu**
el coyote (the coyote)	**au-au-auuuuu**
la culebra, el serpiente (the snake)	**ssst, ssst**

AGUILA, COYOTE, CULEBRA

This is a variation of "Find the Thimble." A child is chosen to be "it" and must leave the room or close his or her eyes for a while. A known object is then hidden somewhere in the class. When the child returns, he or she asks, "**¿Es águila, coyote, o culebra?**" (Is it eagle, coyote, or snake?) These refer to levels in the room. "**Aguila**" means it is hidden up high. "**Coyote**" means it is in the middle range. "**Culebra**" means it is hidden down low. The class tells the level and the child begins to hunt. The class can help the player by calling out "**¡Caliente!**" (hot) if he or she is near the object, or "**¡Frío!**" (cold) if the player is off track.

When the object is found, the player gets to pick the next one to be "it."

¡ARRE!

This is a counting game. When students reach the number 5, or any multiple of 5, they will shout "**¡Arre!**" instead of the number.

Example: **Uno, dos, tres, cuatro ¡Arre!, seis, siete, ocho, nueve, ¡Arre!, once, doce, trece, catorce, ¡Arre!**

ESTOY PENSANDO EN UNA COSA...
(I'm Thinking of Something...)

This guessing game will help kids learn adjectives and classroom vocabulary. The teacher begins by thinking of an object in the room and then gives hints. The students must make their guesses in Spanish.

Example: **la pizarra** (the chalkboard)

Teacher:	**Estoy pensando en una cosa.** I'm thinking of something. **Es un rectángulo.** It's a rectangle.
Class:	(makes a guess)
Teacher:	**Es grande.** It's big.
Class:	(makes a guess)
Teacher:	**Es negro....o verde/ café/ blanco** It is black.... or green/ brown/ white

The class keeps making guesses until they guess right.

DICHOS—PROVERBS

1. **En boca cerrada no entran moscas.**
    (In a closed mouth, flies don't enter.)
    Silence is golden.

2. **Panza llena, corazón contento.**
    (Full tummy, happy heart.)
    Happiness is a full stomach.

3. **Dime con quien andas y te diré quien eres.**
    (Tell me who you go with, and I'll tell you who you are.)
    Birds of a feather flock together.

4. **El que no se atreve, no pasa el mar.**
    (He who doesn't dare, won't cross the sea.)
    Nothing ventured, nothing gained.

5. **Abril lluvioso hace a mayo hermoso.**
    (Rainy April makes a pretty May.)
    April showers bring May flowers.

6. **Poco a poco se va lejos.**
    (Little by little, you go far.)
    Slow and steady wins the race.

7. **Saber es poder.**
    Knowledge is power.

8. **Más vale solo que mal acompañado.**
    Better alone than in bad company.

9. **Cada cabeza es un mundo.**
    (Every head is a world.)
    To each his own.

10. **Si mi tía tuviera ruedas, sería bicicleta.**
    (If my aunt had wheels, she'd be a bicycle.)
    If wishes were horses, beggars would ride.

Chapter Seven

Working with Parents

This chapter will discuss:
- ♦ Working with Parents
- ♦ Notes Home

WORKING WITH PARENTS

Sometimes you will be working with a Spanish-speaking parent. This chapter won't make you fluent, but it will give you some ready phrases to use. Also included are some sample notes home that will make your job easier.

PARENT-TEACHER CONFERENCE

1. **Buenos días (Buenas tardes) Señor/Señora.......**
   Good morning (Good afternoon, evening) Mr./Mrs.....

2. **Es un placer conocerle(s).**
   It's a pleasure to meet you.

3. **Su hijo/hija está en mi clase.**
   Your son/daughter is in my class.

4. **Quiero discutir su progreso.**
   I want to talk about his/her progress.

5. **Es un placer tener a _____ en mi clase.**
   It's a pleasure to have_____ in my class.

6. **Es un buen estudiante. Es una buena estudiante.**
   He/She is a good student.

7. **Es muy trabajador(a).**   (add "a" to the adjective when
   He/She is a hard worker.   speaking about a girl)

47

8. **Es muy listo(a).**
   He/She is very smart.

9. **Es un poco hablador(a).**
   He/She is a bit talkative.

10. **Tiene que trabajar más en _____.**
    He/She has to work more on _____.

11. **Me ayuda mucho en la clase.**
    He/She helps me a lot in the class.

12. **Tiene muchos amigos en la escuela.**
    He/She has many friends at school.

13. **Tiene dificultad en prestar atención.**
    He/She has difficulty paying attention.

14. **Tiene dificultad en quedarse en su asiento.**
    He/She has difficulty staying in his/her seat.

15. **A veces pelea con los otros niños.**
    Sometimes he/she fights with the other children.

16. **¿A que hora se acuesta su hijo/hija?**
    At what time does your son/daughter go to bed?

17. **Necesita acostarse más temprano.**
    He/She needs to go to bed earlier.

18. **Hay que apagar la televisión temprano.**
    The television must be turned off early.

19. **Siempre hace la tarea.**
    He/She always does the homework.

20. **A veces no hace la tarea.**
    Sometimes he/she does not do the homework.

21. **Nunca hace la tarea.**
    He/She never does his/her homework.

22. **Su hijo/hija debe de desayunarse antes de la escuela.**
    Your child should eat breakfast before school.

23. **Gracias por venir a esta conferencia.**
    Thank you for coming to this conference.

THE PARENT MAY ASK YOU SOME QUESTIONS:

1. **¿Cómo va mi hijo/hija en la escuela?***
   How's my son/daughter doing in school?

2. **¿Se porta bien en la clase?**
   Does he/she behave well in class?

3. **¿Está atrasado(a) en algo?**
   Is he/she behind in anything?

4. **¿Cómo puedo ayudarle/la en casa?**
   How can I help him/her at home?

5. **¿Puedo ayudarle en algo aquí en la clase?**
   Can I help you in some way here in the class?

6. **Gracias, maestra(o). ¡Que le vaya bien!**
   Thank you, teacher. May all go well with you.

7. (Teacher's response: **Gracias. Igualmente.**)
   (*Thanks. The same for you.*)

NOTE: Depending on the region, there are several words that mean "child" in Spanish. Here are some of them:
   niño, niña
   muchacho, muchacha
   hijo, hija (you may hear: m'ijo....m'ija)
   chavalito, chavalita
   chamaco, chamaca
   buqui, buquía

NOTES HOME TO PARENTS OR GUARDIANS

FIELD TRIP NOTE

Estimados Padres de familia,

La clase de (*name of teacher*) partirá en un día de campo, el miércoles, el 8 de octubre. Vamos a visitar el zoológico. Nos iremos de la escuela y regresaremos a las horas regulares. No será necesario hacer otros arreglos de transportación para su hijo/hija.

Favor de firmar y regresar la porción al pie de esta carta si su hijo/hija tiene permiso para acompañarnos. Si usted desea ayudarnos con el grupo, sería fantástico.

Atentamente,

(name of teacher) _____

( ) Sí, mi hijo/hija puede visitar el zoológico con su clase el miércoles, el 8 de octubre.

( ) No, mi hijo/hija no puede visitar el zoológico con su clase el miércoles, el 8 de octubre.

Yo, _____ , deseo ayudar con el grupo.

_____
Firma del Padre/Madre/o Guardián

Dear Parents,

(*name of teacher*)'s class will go on a field trip on Wednesday, the 8th of October. We will visit the zoo. We will leave the school and return during regular school hours. It is not necessary for you to make other transportation arrangements for your child.

Please sign and return the bottom section of this letter if your son/daughter has permission to go with us. If you would like to help with the group, that would be great.

Sincerely,

(name of teacher) _____

( )   Yes, my son/daughter has permission to visit the zoo with the class on Wednesday, the 8th of October.

( )   No, my son/daughter does not have permission to visit the zoo with the class on Wednesday, the 8th of October.

I, _____ , want to help with the group.

_____
Signature of parent or guardian

From *Say It in Spanish!* © 1997. Teacher Ideas Press. (800) 237-6124.

OPEN HOUSE NOTE

¡Bienvenidos!

a nuestra fiesta de
"Open House"
a la escuela Madison
viernes, el 10 de septiembre
de las 7:00 hasta las 9:30 p.m.
Habrá refrescos
y la oportunidad de conocer a los maestros.

Welcome!

to our party of
Open House
at Madison School
Friday, the 10th of September
from 7:00 to 9:30 P.M.
There will be refreshments
and the opportunity to meet the teachers.

From *Say It in Spanish!* © 1997. Teacher Ideas Press. (800) 237-6124.

GOOD BEHAVIOR NOTE

Es un placer decirles que _____ (student's name) se ha

destacado en su trabajo de _____ (subject area).

Sigue progresando mucho en la clase.

It is a pleasure to inform you that _____ (student's name)

has done well in his/her work in _____ (subject area).

He/she continues to make progress in class.

From *Say It in Spanish!* © 1997. Teacher Ideas Press. (800) 237-6124.

POOR BEHAVIOR NOTE

_____(student's name) _____ ha tenido dificultad en la clase hoy.

____ Necesita estudiar más _____ (subject area)

____ No presta atención.

____ Pelea con los otros estudiantes.

____ No obedece las reglas de la clase.

Por favor, hable con su hijo/hija acerca de este problema. Con su ayuda, _____

_____ (student's name) puede mejorar su trabajo.

_____(student's name) _____ has had difficulty in class today.

____ Needs to study more _____ (subject area)

____ Does not pay attention.

____ Fights with other students.

____ Does not obey the class rules.

Please speak with your child about this problem. With your help, _____

_____ (student's name) can improve his/her work.

PARENT-TEACHER CONFERENCE NOTE

Estimados padres de familia:

Las conferencias entre los maestros y los padres tendrán lugar la semana que viene. Durante la conferencia habrá la oportunidad de discutir el progreso escolar de su hijo/hija o cualquier problema que haya tenido. Favor de indicar abajo el día y la hora más conveniente para una conferencia con

_____ (name of teacher).

día: lunes   martes   miércoles   jueves   viernes

hora: _____

firma: _____

Dear Parents:

Parent-teacher conferences will take place next week. During the conference there will be the opportunity to discuss the academic progress of your child or any problem he or she may have had. Please indicate below the day and time that is most convenient to attend a conference with

_____ (name of teacher).

day: Monday   Tuesday   Wednesday   Thursday   Friday

time: _____

signed: _____

Chapter Eight
Arts and Crafts

This chapter will discuss:

◆ Art: Bread Dough   Piñatas

             Cascarones   Papel picado

             Bark Painting

BREAD DOUGH ART

This folk art comes from Ecuador. Small ornaments of people, animals or birds are made of bread dough which is then shaped and painted.

Materials:

10 slices of white bread, without crusts
10 teaspoons of white school glue
1 teaspoon of liquid detergent
Tempera or acrylic paint and brushes

Instructions:

1. Tear bread into small pieces in a medium bowl.
2. Add glue and detergent. Stir to blend completely. (Tempera paint may be added to the dough for color, or painted later.)
3. Knead the dough until it is no longer sticky.
4. Roll out the dough on waxed paper.
5. Cut shapes with cookie cutters, scissors, or knife. (Small designs on the dough can be made with toothpicks. Attach pieces with glue.)
6. Brush figures with a mixture of water and glue to prevent shrinkage.
7. Let items dry on waxed paper for at least 12 hours.
8. If color was not added first, paint items now.
9. When dry, varnish or lacquer items for protection.
10. Store unused dough in plastic bags in refrigerator.

CASCARONES

Cascarones are confetti-filled eggs which are meant to be broken over a friend's head! The name comes from the word, "cascar"—"to crack." They are very popular at fiestas and gatherings in the plazas of Mexico, El Salvador, and Guatemala. They are not associated with Easter, although they used to be connected with wishes for a good harvest. Now they bring the "victim" good luck.

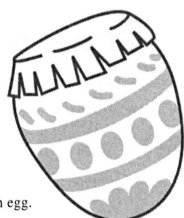

Materials:

whole uncooked eggs
scissors for poking a hole
small bowl
confetti
water color or tempera paints
1" squares of tissue paper
glue

Instructions:

1. Poke a finger-sized hole in the large end of a fresh egg.
2. Empty contents into a bowl.
3. Rinse inside of shell and let dry.
4. When dry, fill egg shells with confetti.
5. Glue tissue paper square over hole.
6. Paint outside of egg.
7. Go find a lucky victim!

BARK PAINTING

Typical bark paintings from Mexico are made on a brownish paper made from fig tree pulp. They are decorated with brightly painted plants, animals, and birds from legends and folktales. This activity uses grocery bags as "bark paper."

Materials:

brown paper shopping bag
bright tempera paints
brushes
warm water
black marker pen

Instructions:

1. Cut the shopping bag to form a large rectangle.
2. Crumple paper into a ball and soak in warm water.
3. Smooth out the paper and flatten.
4. Tear edges of the paper to give a ragged look.
5. Let dry.
6. Pencil in designs.

7. Paint designs with bright colors.
8. When paint is dry, outline in black marker.

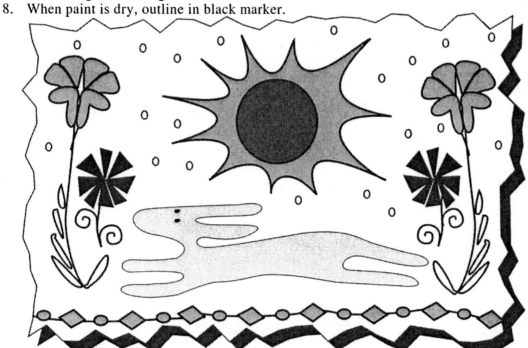

PIÑATAS

Piñatas come in many shapes and sizes. This piñata is cone-shaped and small enough for an individual child to fill with candy.

Materials:

4" circle of tagboard
9" square of tagboard
1 brad
strips of tissue paper 2" in width
glue
string or yarn

Instructions:

1. Overlap opposite ends of square to form a cone.
2. Insert brad 4" from opening of cone to secure it.
3. Cut off point at opening so that it's even around.
4. Double a strip of tissue so that the width is 1".
5. Fringe the tissue paper by cutting on the fold and stopping before you cut to the other side.
6. Glue fringed strips around outside of cone.
7. Cut a 4" circle.
8. Make 1/2" slits one inch apart around the edge of the circle.
9. Fold these inch flaps up.
10. Fill piñata with candy.
11. Glue backs of flaps and insert into cone.
12. Attach string or yarn to hang piñata.

PAPEL PICADO

Mexican fiestas often have decorations of lacy cut papers hung from strings.

Materials:

colored tissue paper pieces, 8 X 11 inches
scissors
paper punch
string

Instructions:

1. Fold the paper as shown:

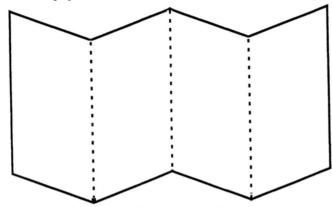

2. Cut out designs along fold, use punch in center.

3. Make a small fold along one side of paper and hang over a string "clothes-line."

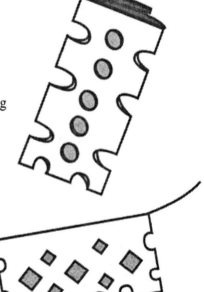

Chapter Nine
Special Days

This chapter will discuss:

♦ Special Days

Los Días de los Muertos	Thanksgiving
Christmas	Valentine's Day
Mother's Day	Cinco de Mayo

DIAS FESTIVOS—HOLIDAYS

Jan. 1	**El Año Nuevo**
Jan. 6	**El Día de los Reyes Magos** (Three Kings Day)
Feb. 14	**El Día de San Valentín**
April 1	**El Día de los Inocentes***
Easter	**Las Pascuas Floridas**
May 5	**El Cinco de Mayo, el día de la independencia de México (de Francia)**
Mother's Day	**El Día de las Madres**
Father's Day	**El Día de los Padres**
July 4	**El Cuatro de Julio, El Día de la Independencia**
Sept. 16	**El Diez y Seis de Septiembre, el día de la independencia de México (de España)**
Oct. 12	**El Día de la Raza** (celebrated by people of Hispanic heritage) **El Día de Cristóbal Colón**
Oct. 31–Nov. 2	**Los Días de los Muertos** (The Days of the Dead)

*Note: In Spain, El Día de los Inocentes is celebrated on December 28th.

Thanksgiving	**El Día de Acción de Gracias**
Dec. 12	**El Día de la Virgen de Guadalupe** (Patron Saint of Mexico)
Dec. 24	**La Nochebuena** (Christmas Eve)
Dec. 25	**La Navidad** (Christmas)
Vacation	**las vacaciones**

LOS DIAS DE LOS MUERTOS— THE DAYS OF THE DEAD

October 31–November 2

In Latin cultures, death is seen as part of the circle of life. It is not shunned, but is talked about openly. From October 31st to November 2nd, Hispanic families gather to remember their loved ones who have died. It is not a scary time, but rather one dedicated to honoring the dead, much like our Memorial Day.

During **Los Días de los Muertos,** The Days of the Dead, families go to the cemetery where their loved ones are buried. Marigold flowers, food, and candles are used to decorate the graves. Special bread and candies are made for this holiday.

A recent picture book by Kathleen Krull, *María Molina and the Days of the Dead*, will help your students learn more about this holiday.

EL DIA DE ACCION DE GRACIAS—THANKSGIVING

Thanksgiving is a good time to discuss plants and animals that are native to the New World. Many of the foods that appear on our holiday tables were cultivated by native peoples long before the Pilgrims landed at Plymouth Rock.

Here are some foods native to Mexico listed with their Spanish and English names:

el guajolote, el pavo	turkey
el tomate	tomato
el aguacate	avocado
el maíz	corn
el chocolate	chocolate
el chili, el chile	chili
los frijoles	beans
la calabaza	squash, pumpkin
la batata	sweet potato

LA NAVIDAD—CHRISTMAS

One colorful custom celebrated in Mexico is **Las Posadas**. During a period of nine days, the people reenact the search made by Mary and Joseph to find a room at the inn, or **la posada**. They form a procession and go from house to house asking for shelter. On the ninth night, they are welcomed into a home and a fiesta is celebrated.

Christmas festivities in Mexico continue until the 6th of January, **el día de los Reyes Magos**, Three Kings Day. One final party is held. **La rosca**, a special bread filled with surprise tokens, is served.

Many homes in the Southwest are decorated with **luminarias.** These are small paper bags, about ¼ filled with sand, holding a lit candle. The bags are placed along walks, driveways, and on rooftops.

Your class could have its own posada procession by going from class to class singing Christmas songs in Spanish. The class returns and has a fiesta and breaks a piñata filled with candy.

A good resource for Christmas customs and songs is *La Navidad: Christmas in Spain and Latin America*, by Agnes M. Brady, published by National Textbook Company.

Christmas vocabulary:

¡Feliz Navidad!	Merry Christmas
La Nochebuena	Christmas Eve
el árbol de Navidad	the Christmas tree
las luces navideñas	Christmas lights
El Nacimiento	the Nativity scene
La Santa Familia	The Holy Family
Belén	Bethlehem
los Reyes Magos	the Wise Men
la estrella	the star
los regalos	the presents
las fiestas	the parties
las luminarias	the candle lights
cascabeles	jingle bells
Santa Clos	Santa Claus
los venados	the reindeer
el Polo Norte	the North Pole
¡Feliz Año Nuevo!	Happy New Year!

EL DIA DE SAN VALENTIN—VALENTINE'S DAY

Here are some sweet messages to write on Valentine cards:

¡Feliz Día de San Valentín!	Happy Valentine's Day!
¡Amigos para siempre!	Friends forever!
¿Me quieres?	Do you love me?
Te amo / Te quiero	I love you
¡Es bueno ser amigos!	It's nice to be friends!
Mucho cariño	Much love
Besos y abrazos	Hugs and kisses
¿Serás mío/mía?	Will you be mine?
Eres mi novio/novia	You're my boyfriend/girlfriend
Eres mi ......favorito/a	You are my favorite.....

EL DIA DE LAS MADRES—MOTHER'S DAY

In Mexico, Mother's Day is always celebrated on the 10th of May. In the United States it is the first Sunday in May. Here is a poem for kids to learn for **El Día de las Madres**. This poem also works well in sign language.

Amor de mamá	*Mama Love*
Amo a mi mamá	I love my mama
Mi mamá me ama a mí	My mama loves me
Su sonrisa es el sol	Her smile is the sun
Sus besos son las estrellas	Her kisses are the stars
Su amor es mi arco iris	Her love is my rainbow
Amo a mi mamá	I love my mama
Mi mamá me ama a mí	My mama loves me

Children can make cards with their own Mother's Day greetings:

Te quiero, Mamá.	I love you, Mom.
Eres la mejor, Mamá.	You're the best, Mom.
¡Mi mamá es fantástica!	My mom is fantastic!
¡Feliz día de las madres!	Happy Mother's Day!
Mucho amor para Abuelita.	Much love to Grandma.

CINCO DE MAYO—THE FIFTH OF MAY

Mexico's official independence day is September 16th when she celebrates her independence from Spain in 1810. May 5th, **Cinco de Mayo,** celebrates her liberation from France.

In 1862, Mexico's President was the great reformer, Benito Juárez. He tried to unify the country against the forces of poverty and bad government. At that time, the armed forces of Mexico were very weak. There was confusion among the generals. Mexico was facing a huge debt to several countries in Europe and had few resources with which to repay it.

Under the guise of helping Mexico, France sent part of its army to Mexico. But instead of helping, France took possession of the port of Vera Cruz and began an invasion of the country. The French army was large and well-equipped, the best in the world at that time.

Of course, the Mexicans resented having a foreign government in their country. So, in spite of their poor rag-tag army, they decided to fight back. The desire for a free Mexico gave them courage against all the odds.

On the fifth of May, 1862, in the town of Puebla, a decisive battle was fought. Under the direction of a young general, Ignacio Zaragoza, the Mexican army defeated the French army. It was only one battle victory, but it served to inspire other Mexican units in the country. They saw that it was possible to fight the superior French army.

Napoleon III had to send more troops to Mexico until the country was under control. Napoleon sent Maximilian to serve as Emperor of Mexico. But the desire for freedom was pulsing through the country. Five years later, after many more battles, the Mexicans finally won their independence. Maximilian was executed, and the French were kicked out.

Cinco de Mayo represents an opportunity to celebrate liberty. Many cities in the U.S. have fiestas and parades to mark the Fifth of May, even though it is a Mexican holiday. Our own Independence Day, July 4th, is celebrated in Norway, France, and other countries for the same reason. The liberty of a people is always cause for celebration.

Some other Independence Days in Latin America:

September 15: Costa Rica, El Salvador, Guatemala, Honduras, and Nicaragua
September 16: Mexico
November 3: Panama
May 20: Cuba

ART: LA BANDERA—The Flag

According to an Aztec legend, the god Huitzilopoxtli (wee-chee-lo-POSH-lee) told his people that they must move southward and settle at the spot where they saw an eagle devouring a snake. After wandering for a long time, the Aztecs saw this event on an island located in the lake Texcoco (tes-CO-co). Here they built their city, called Tenochtitlán (teh-nok-cheet-LAN). It would become today's Mexico City. Gradually, the lake was filled in. All that remains of the original waterway is Lake Xochimilco (so-chee-MIL-co), known for its floating gardens.

The colors of the Mexican flag are (from left to right) green, white, and red. The green represents "independence," white is for "religion," and red is for "union." In the center we see the eagle devouring a snake on a cactus. Flag day in Mexico is February 24.

Vocabulary to practice:

la bandera mexicana	the Mexican flag
verde	green
blanco	white
rojo	red
el águila	the eagle
la serpiente	the serpent
el nopal	the cactus

¿Cuáles son los colores de la bandera mexicana?
What are the colors of the Mexican flag?

Son verde, blanco, y rojo.
They are green, white, and red.

¿Qué hay en el centro de la bandera?
What is there in the center of the flag?

Hay un águila
There is an eagle

comiendo una serpiente
eating a snake

sobre un nopal.
on a cactus.

Flag on page 68.

From *Say It in Spanish!* © 1997. Teacher Ideas Press. (800) 237-6124.

Chapter Ten
Two Flannel Board Stories

This chapter includes two
flannel board stories:

- ◆ "El jardín"
- ◆ "El león y el grillo"

EL JARDIN

**Un verano, Tomás sembró un jardín. Era un jardín
especial para sus amigos.
Ardilla le miró sembrar tomates.
Conejo le miró sembrar lechuga.
Pájaro le miró sembrar girasoles.
Tomás regaba el jardín cada día. Crecieron los tomates.
Creció la lechuga. Crecieron los girasoles.
"¡Bien!" dijo Tomás. "Mi jardín está listo."
Vino Ardilla. Se comió los tomates.
Vino Conejo. Se comió la lechuga.
Vino Pájaro. Se comió las semillas de los girasoles.
"¡Bravo!" dijo Tomás. "Mi jardín estaba perfecto para
mis amigos Ardilla, Conejo, y Pájaro!"**

Translation:

A boy plants a special garden of tomatoes, lettuce, and sunflowers. His friends, Squirrel, Rabbit,
and Bird come along and eat it all up.

From *Turtle Magazine for Preschoolers*, copyright © 1995 by Children's Better Health Institute, Benjamin Franklin
Literary & Medical Society, Inc. Indianapolis, Indiana. Used by permission.

From *Say It in Spanish!* © 1997. Teacher Ideas Press. (800) 237-6124.

From *Say It in Spanish!* © 1997. Teacher Ideas Press. (800) 237-6124.

From *Say It in Spanish!* © 1997. Teacher Ideas Press. (800) 237-6124.

From *Say It in Spanish!* © 1997. Teacher Ideas Press. (800) 237-6124.

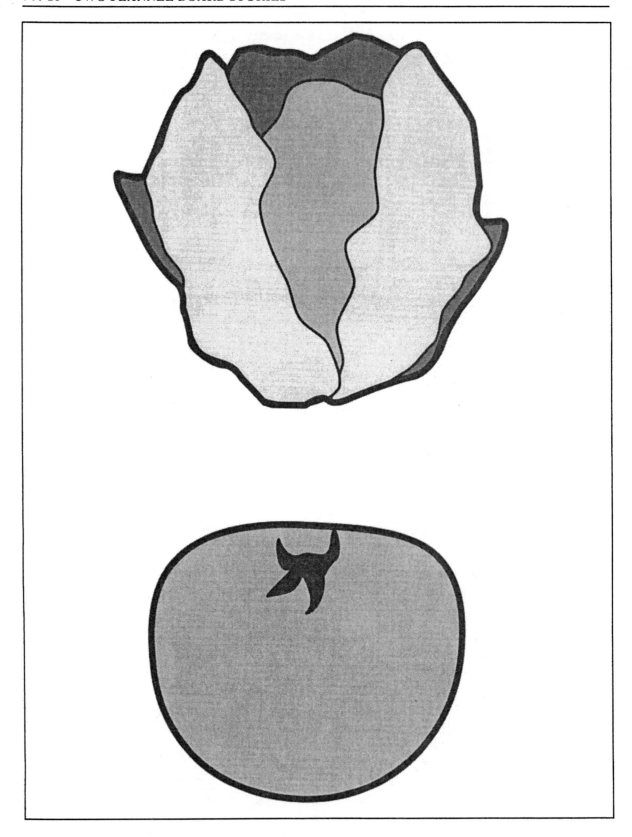

From *Say It in Spanish!* © 1997. Teacher Ideas Press. (800) 237-6124.

From *Say It in Spanish!* © 1997. Teacher Ideas Press. (800) 237-6124.

EL LEON Y EL GRILLO

Un día León caminaba por la selva.
"¡Hola!" dijo el loro.
"¡Hola!" dijo el mono.
Grillo no dijo "¡Hola!" Estaba cantando en su jardín.
"No eres muy cortés," dijo León. "Vamos a correr a la
roca grande. Si ganas, te perdono tu falta de cortesía.
¿Listo? ¡Vamos!"
León comenzó a correr. Grillo brincó a su espalda.
León no vio a grillo. "¡Voy a ganar!" dijo León.
Grillo brincó a la cabeza de León. Cuando se acercaron
a la roca grande, allí brincó Grillo."
"¡Hola!" dijo Grillo.
"¡Olé! ¡Grillo gana!" dijeron el loro y el mono.
"¿Qué pasó?" dijo León.

Translation:

One day Lion was walking through the jungle.
"Hello!" said the parrot.
"Hello!" said the monkey.
Cricket did not say "Hello!" He was singing in his garden.
"You're not very polite," said Lion. "We will race to
the big rock. If you win, I will pardon your bad manners.
Ready? Go!"
Lion began to run. Cricket jumped onto his back. Lion
did not see Cricket. "I'm going to win!" said Lion.
Cricket jumped onto Lion's head. When they neared the big
rock, off jumped Cricket.
"Hello!" said Cricket.
"Hooray! Cricket wins!" said the parrot and the monkey.
"How did that happen?" said Lion.

Used by permission of *Highlights for Children, Inc.* Columbus, Ohio. © Copyright 1993.

© 1995 Lori Trimboli

From *Say It in Spanish!* © 1997. Teacher Ideas Press. (800) 237-6124.

From *Say It in Spanish!* © 1997. Teacher Ideas Press. (800) 237-6124.

From *Say It in Spanish!* © 1997. Teacher Ideas Press. (800) 237-6124.

From *Say It in Spanish!* © 1997. Teacher Ideas Press. (800) 237-6124.

From *Say It in Spanish!* © 1997. Teacher Ideas Press. (800) 237-6124.

Chapter Eleven

Songs

This chapter includes the
following songs:

- Fray Felipe
- Buenos días
- Diez amigos
- Adiós
- Los pollitos dicen
- La piñata
- Vengan a ver mi chacra

FRAY FELIPE AND BUENOS DIAS

(Both songs to the tune: "Are You Sleeping, Brother John?")

FRAY FELIPE ("Fray" is pronounced "Fry")

Fray Felipe,	Brother Philip,
Fray Felipe.	Brother Philip.
¿Duermes tú?	Are you sleeping?
¿Duermes tú?	Are you sleeping?
Toca la campana.	The bell is ringing.
Toca la campana.	The bell is ringing.
Tin, tan, tin.	Ding, dong, ding.
Tin, tan, tin.	Ding, dong, ding.

BUENOS DIAS (GOOD MORNING)

Buenos días,	Good morning,
Buenos días,	Good morning,
¿Cómo estás?	How are you?
¿Cómo estás?	How are you?
Muy bien, gracias.	Very well, thank you.
Muy bien, gracias.	Very well, thank you.
¿Y usted?	And you?
¿Y usted?	And you?

(Text continues on page 87.)

FRAY FELIPE

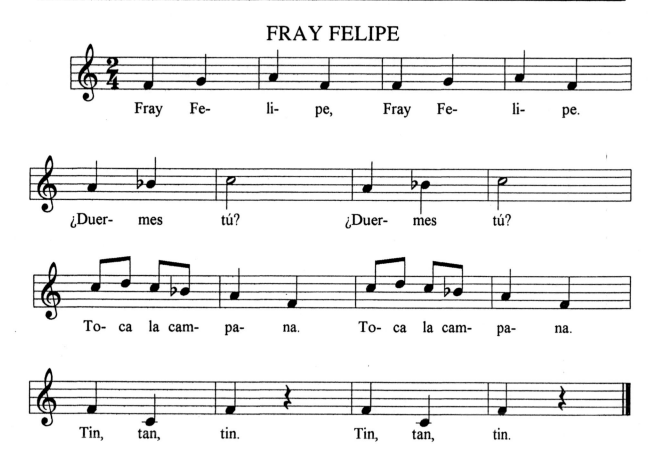

Fray Fe- li- pe, Fray Fe- li- pe.

¿Duer- mes tú? ¿Duer- mes tú?

To- ca la cam- pa- na. To- ca la cam- pa- na.

Tin, tan, tin. Tin, tan, tin.

From *Say It in Spanish!* © 1997. Teacher Ideas Press. (800) 237-6124.

BUENOS DIAS

From *Say It in Spanish!* © 1997. Teacher Ideas Press. (800) 237-6124.

DIEZ AMIGOS AND ADIOS

(Both songs to the tune: "Ten Little Indians")

DIEZ AMIGOS*

Uno, dos, tres amigos,
cuatro, cinco, seis amigos,
siete, ocho, nueve amigos,
diez amigos son.
Diez, nueve, ocho amigos,
siete, seis, cinco amigos,
cuatro, tres, dos amigos,
un amigo es.   (notice how verb becomes singular)

---

*Other words can be substituted for "**amigos,**" (friends) such as: **patitos, gatitos, ositos,** etc. (ducks) (kittens) (bears)

¡ADIOS! (SO LONG!)

¡Adiós, ya nos vamos!	So long, now we're going!
¡Adiós, ya nos vamos!	So long, now we're going!
Otra vez practicamos	Once again we will practice
Mucho español.	Lots of Spanish.

(Text continues on page 90.)

DIEZ AMIGOS

From *Say It in Spanish!* © 1997. Teacher Ideas Press. (800) 237-6124.

¡ADIOS!

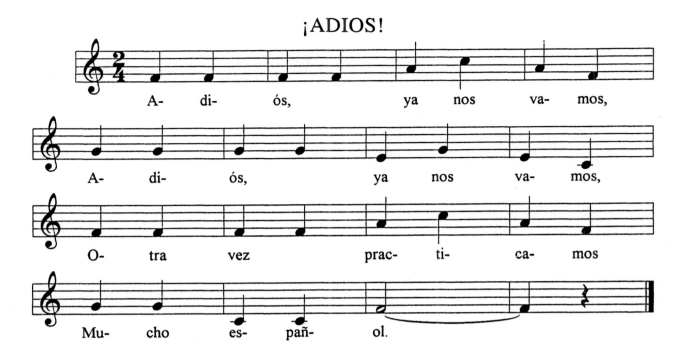

A- di- ós, ya nos va- mos,

A- di- ós, ya nos va- mos,

O- tra vez prac- ti- ca- mos

Mu- cho es- pañ- ol.

From *Say It in Spanish!* © 1997. Teacher Ideas Press. (800) 237-6124.

LOS POLLITOS DICEN

(A traditional song from Mexico)

Los pollitos dicen,	Little chickens cry out
"pío, pío, pío"	"pío, pío, pío"
cuando tienen hambre,	when they're feeling hungry,
cuando tienen frío.	when they're feeling cold.
La gallina busca	Mother hen goes looking
el maíz y trigo,	for the corn and wheat
y les da comida,	and she gives them dinner,
y les presta abrigo.	and she keeps them warm. (lends them a coat)

LOS POLLITOS DICEN

From *Say It in Spanish!* © 1997. Teacher Ideas Press. (800) 237-6124.

LA PIÑATA

This is one of many variations of piñata songs. There are other verses, but for now, teach just the chorus.

Hang the candy-filled piñata from a beam using a rope. One end of the rope must hang down so someone can manipulate the piñata up and down. A child is chosen, blindfolded, and turned around a few times. Then the child gets a stick and tries to hit the piñata. All the while, the other kids sing this song. Three swings, and a new player is chosen.

¡Dale, dale, dale!	Hit it, hit it, hit it!
No pierdas el tino.	Don't lose your aim.
Porque si lo pierdes,	Because if you lose it,
Pierdes el camino.	You'll lose the way.
¡Dale, dale, dale!	
No pierdas el tino.	
Que de la distancia	For with this distance
Se pierde el camino.	You lose the way.
¡Dale, dale, dale!	
No pierdas el tino.	
Mide la distancia	Measure the distance
Que hay en el camino.	There is on the way.

LA PIÑATA

From *Say It in Spanish!* © 1997. Teacher Ideas Press. (800) 237-6124.

VENGAN A VER MI CHACRA

("Chacra" is a farm in Argentina.)

Vengan a ver mi chacra que es hermosa,
Vengan a ver mi chacra que es hermosa,
El perrito hace así: guau-guau-guau:
El perrito hace así: guau-guau-guau.
¡O Va camarad! ¡o va camarad!
¡O va, o va, o va!
¡O va camarad! ¡o va camarad!
¡O va, o va, o va!

(other animals)

El perrito hace así:	¡guau, guau! (wow-wow)
El gatito hace así:	¡miau, miau!
El caballo hace así:	¡Ji-ji-ji-ji! (hee-hee)
El burrito hace así:	¡Ji-ja! (hee-ha)
La gallina hace así:	¡Clo-clo-clo!
El patito hace así:	¡Cua-cua-cua!
La oveja hace así:	¡Maa-maa!
Y la vaca hace así:	¡Muu-muu!
Y el gallo hace así:	¡Ki-kiri-kí!

VENGAN A VER MI CHACRA

Ven- gan a ver mi cha- cra que es her- mo - sa,

Ven- gan a ver mi cha- cra que es her- mo - sa,

El per- rri- to- ha- ce a- sí: guau-guau-guau:

El per- rri- to- ha- ce a- sí: guau-guau-guau. ¡O

Va, ca- ma rad! ¡o va, ca-ma rad! ¡O va, o va, o va! ¡O

va, ca-marad! ¡o va, ca-ma rad! ¡O va, o va o va!

From *Say It in Spanish!* © 1997. Teacher Ideas Press. (800) 237-6124.

Chapter Twelve

A Play:
The Coyote and the Old Dog
(El coyote y el perro viejo)

ACTING OUT LANGUAGE

One of the best ways to learn a language is to act out what you are saying. The combination of body movements and story context help make the language come to life. When you learn "tengo hambre" together with the action of patting the tummy, then the words "I'm hungry" take on real meaning.

This play is based on a folktale from Mexico. But it also has origins in a tale from the Brothers Grimm, "Old Sultan." Folktales have a way of traveling around the world.

"The Coyote and the Old Dog" has been performed by students in the third and fourth grades, some with little or no Spanish training. Teachers and students alike had no trouble presenting this play in Spanish. The kids had fun and learned quickly.

The play is given here in both languages. The sets and costuming have been kept to a minimum. There are eight speaking parts. Students who don't have a speaking part can be part of the chorus and sing the songs. The melodies are provided in the chapter on songs.

¡Buena suerte!   Break a leg!

THE COYOTE AND THE OLD DOG

(El coyote y el perro viejo)

by Marianne Mitchell

Cast:	ANIMALS OF THE RANCH
	GUARDIAN
	TURKEY
	CAT
	ROOSTER
	COW
	COYOTE
	RANCHER
	WIFE OF RANCHER

Setting: A ranch in Mexico or in the southwestern United States. There are two bales of hay to the right, a tree in the foreground to the left.

As the curtain rises: The ANIMALS OF THE RANCH are standing in a semi-circle at the back. GUARDIAN is sleeping in center stage.

SCENE 1

ANIMALS: (*singing*) (tune: "Vengan a ver mi chacra")
"Come to my ranch, it is so beautiful,
Come to my ranch, it is so beautiful,
And the kitty goes like this: meow, meow, meow,
And the rooster goes like this: Cock-adoodle-do!
Oh, come over here, oh come over here,
And join us in our play!
Oh, come over here, oh come over here,
And join us in our play!"

TURKEY: (*steps forward*)
Welcome to our ranch! I am the prize turkey. This is Guardian, the old dog.

GUARDIAN: (*wakes up, looks at the audience, goes back to sleep*)

TURKEY:
Guardian is really old.

CAT: (*steps forward*)
He used to bark a lot.

EL COYOTE Y EL PERRO VIEJO

(The Coyote and the Old Dog)

por Marianne Mitchell

Los personajes:	ANIMALES DEL RANCHO
	GUARDIAN
	GUAJOLOTE
	GATO
	GALLO
	VACA
	COYOTE
	RANCHERO
	ESPOSA DEL RANCHERO

Escenario: Un rancho en México o en el suroeste de los Estados Unidos. Hay dos bultos de paja a la derecha, un árbol en el proscenio a la izquierda.

Al subir el telón: Los ANIMALES DEL RANCHO están parados en un semi-círculo al fondo. GUARDIAN está dormido en el centro.

ESCENA 1

ANIMALES: (cantan) (melodía: "Vengan a ver mi chacra")
"Vengan a ver mi rancho, que es bonito,
Vengan a ver mi rancho, que es bonito,
Y el gato dice así: Miau, miau, miau,
Y el gallo dice así: ¡Ki-ki-ri-ki!
¡O, vengan acá, o vengan acá,
Que vamos a jugar!
¡O vengan acá, o vengan acá,
Que vamos a jugar!"

GUAJOLOTE: (*da un paso al frente*) ¡Bienvenidos a nuestro rancho! Yo soy el guajolote premiado. Aquí está Guardián, el perro viejo.

GUARDIAN: (*se despierta, mira al público, vuelve a dormir*)

GUAJOLOTE:
Guardián tiene muchos años.

GATO: (*da un paso al frente*)
Antes ladraba mucho.

ROOSTER: (*steps forward—stutters*)
He used to-to-to-to-to run a lot.

COW: (*steps forward*)
Now he hardly moooooooves.

TURKEY:
A coyote lives near here.

CAT:
I'm not afraid of coyote.

ROOSTER:
I am! And who's g-g-g-g-g-gonna defend the ranch?

TURKEY:
This lazy old sleepyhead! (*boots Guardian gently*)

(*COW, ROOSTER, CAT, and TURKEY join the other animals in the back. All sit down.*)

SCENE 2

(*Enter RANCHER and WIFE. GUARDIAN continues sleeping.*)

COYOTE: (*off stage*)
Yow-ow-ow-ow-aoooooooo!

WIFE:
Listen! It's the coyote! He wants to attack the animals.

RANCHER:
Yes, but Guardian is here.

WIFE:
That dog isn't worth anything. He's always sleeping.

RANCHER:
It's true. He's very old.

WIFE:
He's ugly and never does a thing. I want a young dog.

RANCHER:
But what will we do with Guardian?

WIFE:
Let's not feed him anymore. He'll soon go to another house. Go on! Get out of here, sleepyhead!
(*She shoos the dog away. Guardian sadly exits to the right. RANCHER and WIFE exit.*)

GALLO: (*da un paso al frente—es tartamudo*)
Antes co-co-co-co-rría mucho.

VACA: (*da un paso al frente*)
Ahora duerme muuuuucho.

GUAJOLOTE:
Un coyote vive cerca de aquí.

GATO:
No tengo miedo del coyote.

GALLO:
¡Yo sí! ¿Y ki-ki-ki-ki-quién nos defiende?

GUAJOLOTE:
¡Este perro dormilón! (*da una patada al perro*)

(*VACA, GALLO, GATO y GUAJOLOTE se reúnen con los otros animales en el fondo. Todos se sientan.*)

ESCENA 2

(*Entra RANCHERO y ESPOSA DEL RANCHERO. GUARDIAN duerme.*)

COYOTE: (*fuera de la escena*)
¡Aúúúúú! ¡Aúúúúú!

ESPOSA:
¡Oye! Es el coyote. Quiere atacar a los animales.

RANCHERO:
Sí, pero Guardián está aquí.

ESPOSA:
Este perro no vale para nada. Siempre está dormido.

RANCHERO:
Es verdad. Es muy viejo.

ESPOSA:
Es feo y no hace nada. Quiero un perro joven.

RANCHERO:
¿Qué haremos con Guardián?

ESPOSA:
No le daremos más comida. Pronto se irá a otra casa. ¡Vete, vete, Dormilón!
(Hace un gesto de correr al perro. Guardián sale muy triste a la derecha)

SCENE 3

Setting: On the road, near the ranch. The action takes place on the apron. A tree is to the left. GUARDIAN is at the right, crying. COYOTE is to the left, under the tree.

GUARDIAN: (*crying*)
Boo-hoo! Boo-hoo! Boo-hoo!

COYOTE:
What's happening? Who's crying?

GUARDIAN: (*crying more*)
Boo-hoo! Boo-hoo! Boo-hoo!

COYOTE:
It's my friend, the old dog. I'll go talk to him. (*goes over to GUARDIAN*)

GUARDIAN:
What am I going to do? Boo-hoo! Boo-hoo!

COYOTE:
Hello, friend! What's the matter? Why are you crying?

GUARDIAN:
My masters don't want me any more. They say I don't defend the ranch. They won't feed me any more!

COYOTE:
That's ridiculous! I stopped coming to the ranch because you were so brave.

GUARDIAN:
But now I have to find another home. And who wants an old dog like me?

COYOTE: (*takes a step to the left, thinking*)
With an old dog it's easier to rob.
With a young dog, it'll be a job.
(*moves back to the center toward GUARDIAN*) I have an idea. I'll come to the ranch tonight. You chase me away. I won't steal anything.

GUARDIAN: (*gets up*)
Are you telling the truth? You won't steal anything?

COYOTE: (*seriously to the dog*)
I promise you. Nothing! (*turns, smiles at the audience*) I promise you nothing!

(*GUARDIAN hears this with shock, shakes his fist at COYOTE. COYOTE doesn't see him. Exit GUARDIAN and COYOTE.*)

ESCENA 3

Escenario: En el camino, cerca del rancho. La acción toma lugar en el proscenio. Un árbol está a la izquierda. GUARDIAN está a la derecha llorando. COYOTE está a la izquierda, descansando debajo del árbol.

GUARDIAN: (*llora*)
¡Uu-ju-ju-uu!

COYOTE:
¿Qué pasa? ¿Quién está llorando?

GUARDIAN: (*sigue llorando*)
¡Uu-ju-ju-uu!

COYOTE:
Es mi amigo el perro viejo. Voy a hablar con él. (*Va hacia Guardián*)

GUARDIAN:
¿Qué voy a hacer? ¡Uu-ju-ju-uu!

COYOTE:
¡Hola, amigo! ¿Qué pasa? ¿Por qué lloras?

GUARDIAN:
Mis amos no me quieren más. Dicen que no defiendo el rancho. ¡No me darán más comida!

COYOTE:
¡Es ridículo! Yo no vengo más al rancho porque eres tan bravo.

GUARDIAN:
Pero tengo que buscar otra casa. ¿Y quién quiere un perro viejo como yo?

COYOTE: (*da un paso a la izquierda, pensando*)
Con un perro viejo, es más fácil robar.
Con un perro joven, tengo que trabajar.
(*pasa al centro hacia el perro*) Tengo una idea. Esta noche vengo al rancho. Tú me corres del rancho. No robo nada.

GUARDIAN: (*se levanta*)
¿Dices la verdad? ¿No vas a robar nada?

COYOTE: (*en serio al perro*)
Nada. Te lo prometo. (*sonríe al público*) ¡Nada te prometo!

(*GUARDIAN hace cara de sorpresa, luego hace un gesto de indignación a COYOTE. COYOTE no lo ve. Salen los dos.*)

SCENE 4

Setting: At the ranch. The ANIMALS are seated in the back. The bales of hay are to the right. GUARDIAN enters, moves to the center and speaks to the audience.

GUARDIAN:
It is night at the ranch. Soon Coyote will come. Is he my friend or my enemy? We'll see.
(*He hides behind the bales of hay.*) (*Enter COYOTE looking for his dinner.*)

COYOTE:
Mmmmmm! I'm hungry! I'd like a turkey dinner.
(*While the ANIMALS sing, COYOTE goes all over looking for TURKEY. He stops behind TURKEY at the end of the song.*)

ANIMALS: (*they sit as they sing*) (tune: "Are You Sleeping, Brother John?")
"Are you sleeping?
Are you sleeping?
Dear old dog!
Dear old dog!
Coyote's gonna get him,
Are you gonna let him?
Pum, pum, pum.
Pum, pum, pum."

COYOTE: (*grabs TURKEY*)
Aha! You're mine!

TURKEY:
He's going to eat me! Save me! Save me!

GUARDIAN: (*attacks COYOTE*)
Arf! Arf! Arf!

COYOTE: (*lets go of TURKEY, runs off stage*)
Ay! Ay! Ay! (*enter RANCHER and WIFE who see everything*)

RANCHER: (*to GUARDIAN*)
What a good dog you are! How brave you are! Don't leave the ranch!

WIFE:
Oh, Guardian, come here! Forgive me! Here's a nice tortilla with meat for you. (*she gives him a tortilla and he eats it*)

COYOTE: (*speaking from stage left*)
Look at him! He has food and I have nothing!

ANIMALS: (*they stand and shout*)
Hooray for Guardian! Hooray for Guardian!

ESCENA 4

Escenario: En el rancho. Los ANIMALES están sentados al fondo. Los bultos de paja están a la derecha. GUARDIAN entra, pasa al centro, y habla al público.

GUARDIAN:
Es de noche en el rancho. Pronto viene Coyote. ¿Es mi amigo o mi enemigo? Vamos a ver.
(*Se esconde detrás de los bultos de paja.*) (*Entra COYOTE en busca de comida.*)

COYOTE:
¡Mmmmm! ¡Tengo hambre! Quiero una comida de guajolote.
(*Mientras cantan los ANIMALES, COYOTE pasa por todas partes en busca de GUAJOLOTE. Se para detrás de GUAJOLOTE al final de la canción.*)

ANIMALES: (*están sentados y cantan*) (melodía: "Fray Felipe")
"Perro viejo,
perro viejo,
¿Duermes tú?
¿Duermes tú?
Pobre guajolote,
Viene el coyote,
Pum, pum, pum.
Pum, pum, pum."

COYOTE: (*agarra el guajolote*)
¡Ay ¡Eres mío!

GUAJOLOTE:
¡Me va a comer! ¡Ayúdenme! ¡Ayúdenme!

GUARDIAN: (*ataca al coyote*)
¡Rauf! ¡Rauf! ¡Rauf!

COYOTE: (*suelta al guajolote, corre de la escena*)
¡Ayy! ¡Ayy! ¡Ayy! (*salen el RANCHERO y la ESPOSA DEL RANCHERO y ven todo*)

RANCHERO: (*a GUARDIAN*)
¡Qué buen perro eres! ¡Qué bravo eres! ¡No te vayas del rancho!

ESPOSA:
O, Guardián, ¡ven acá! ¡Perdóname! Aquí tengo una tortilla con carne para ti. (*le da una tortilla y el perro come*)

COYOTE: (*habla desde la izquierda del escenario*)
¡Mírenle! El tiene comida y yo no tengo nada.

ANIMALES: (*se levantan y gritan a la misma vez*)
¡Qué viva Guardián! ¡Qué viva Guardián!

ANIMALS: (*singing*) (tune: "Vengan a ver mi chacra")
"Come to my ranch, it is so beautiful,
Come to my ranch, it is so beautiful,
And the turkey goes like this....."

TURKEY: (*steps forward*)
Thank you, Guardian!

ANIMALS:
"....and the guard dog goes like this..."

GUARDIAN: (*steps forward*)
You're welcome!

ANIMALS:
"...and coyote goes like this..."

COYOTE: (*from the side, pointing to the old dog*)
He may be old, but he's no fool!

ANIMALS: (*singing*)
"Oh, come over here, oh, come over here,
And join us in our play!
Oh, come over here, oh, come over here,
And join us in our play!"

—THE END—

ANIMALES: (*cantan*) (melodía: "Vengan a ver mi chacra")
"Vengan a ver mi rancho, que es bonito,
Vengan a ver mi rancho, que es bonito,
Y el guajolote dice así......"

GUAJOLOTE: (*da un paso al frente*)
¡Gracias, Guardián!

ANIMALES:
"...y el perro dice así...."

GUARDIAN: (*da un paso al frente*)
De nada.

ANIMALES:
"...y el coyote dice así..."

COYOTE: (*desde el lado, indica el perro viejo*)
¡Viejo es, pero bobo no es!

ANIMALES: (*siguen cantando*)
"¡O vengan acá , o vengan acá,
Que vamos a jugar!
¡O vengan acá, o vengan acá,
Que vamos a jugar!"

—TELON—

APPENDIX A
Answers to Practice Exercises

Chapter 2, p. 8 (using **el** and **la**)

la ventana	**la puerta**	**el gato**	**el lápiz**
el maestro	**la oficina**	**la clase**	**la mano**
el zapato	**el mapa**	**el número**	**la mujer**

Chapter 2, p. 9 (making plurals)

los gatos blancos
las clases grandes
unos niños inteligentes
unas muchachas altas
¿Cuáles libros?

Chapter 2, pp. 10-11 (showing agreement)

libro abierto	open book
niños pequeños	small children
papeles nuevos	new papers
clase grande	big class
día caliente	hot day
zapatos viejos	old shoes
maestra simpática	nice teacher (female)
maestro simpático	nice teacher (male)
cuentos interesantes	interesting stories

Chapter 2, pp. 12-13 (plural nouns and adjectives)

niño—niños	silla—sillas
olor—olores	papel—papeles
tren—trenes	pez—peces
clase—clases	luz—luces
día—días	noche—noches
maestra—maestras	pelota—pelotas
hermano—hermanos	verde—verdes
joven—jóvenes	canción —canciones
bandera—banderas	azul—azules
flor—flores	árbol—árboles
lápiz—lápices	feliz—felices

Chapter 2, pp. 15-16 (using **al** and **del**, possession)

1. **Es la mesa del estudiante.**
2. **Es el lápiz de la maestra.**
3. **Me gustan los cuentos de los niños.**
4. **Voy a la oficina.**
5. **Voy al parque.**
6. **Me gusta enseñar a los niños.**
7. **Es de Robbyn.**
8. **Es de Jackson.**
9. **Es de la maestra.**
10. **Es del maestro.**
11. **Es del niño.**
12. **mi lápiz**
13. **nuestra escuela**
14. **sus amigos/amigas**
15. **tu silla**

Chapter 2, p. 16 (using **hay**)

1. **Hay treinta estudiantes en mi clase.**
2. **¿Hay un maestro/una maestra?**
3. **No hay tiza.**
4. **¿Cuántos libros hay?**
5. **¿Cuántos días hay en una semana?**

Chapter 3, p. 23 (verbs **TENER, SER, ESTAR**)

1. **Tengo un libro.**
2. **Tienes/Tiene mi lápiz.**
3. **Tiene ocho años.**
4. **Tenemos hambre.**
5. **Mis gatos tienen miedo.**
6. **Soy la maestra.**
7. **Somos de Guatemala.**
8. **Juan es mi amigo.**
9. **María es mexicana.**
10. **La casa es de adobe.**
11. **¿Estás/Está triste?**
12. **Estoy enfermo.**
13. **¿Dónde está José?**
14. **Está en la oficina.**
15. **Los niños están sucios.**

Chapter 3, pp. 23-24 (verbs **LLAMARSE, GUSTAR, IR**)

1. **¿Cómo te llamas? ¿Cómo se llama?**
2. **Me llamo Rita.**
3. **Mi escuela se llama Adams.**
4. **Nos llamamos "Los Tigres."**
5. **¿Cómo se llaman tus padres?**
6. **Me gusta el color rojo.**
7. **¿Te gustan los gatos?**
8. **No le gusta bailar.**
9. **Nos gusta estudiar.**
10. **Me gustan los sábados.**
11. **Voy a la oficina.**
12. **Vamos a cantar.**
13. **Mateo va a la escuela.**
14. **¿Vas a la fiesta? (or ...¿Va usted a la fiesta?)**
15. **Ellos no van conmigo.**

Chapter 3, p. 26 (Present tense of **-AR, -ER, -IR** verbs)

1. **(yo) estudio, (tú) estudias, (usted, él, ella) estudia, (nosotros) estudiamos, (ustedes, ellos, ellas) estudian**

2. **(yo) camino, (tú) caminas, (usted, él, ella) camina, (nosotros) caminamos, (ustedes, ellos, ellas) caminan**

3. (yo) **canto**, (tú) **cantas**, (usted, él, ella) **canta**, (nosotros) **cantamos**, (ustedes, ellos, ellas) **cantan**

4. (yo) **como**, (tú) **comes**, (usted, él, ella) **come**, (nosotros) **comemos**, (ustedes, ellos, ellas) **comen**

5. (yo) **leo**, (tú) **lees**, (usted, él, ella) **lee**, (nosotros) **leemos**, (ustedes, ellos, ellas) **leen**

6. (yo) **corro**, (tú) **corres**, (usted, él, ella) **corre**, (nosotros) **corremos**, (ustedes, ellos, ellas) **corren**

7. (yo) **escribo**, (tú) **escribes**, (usted, él, ella) **escribe**, (nosotros) **escribimos**, (ustedes, ellos, ellas) **escriben**

8. (yo) **decido**, (tú) **decides**, (usted, él, ella) **decide**, (nosotros) **decidimos**, (ustedes, ellos, ellas) **deciden**

APPENDIX B
Useful Vocabulary

LOS COLORES—Colors

rojo	red
azul	blue
amarillo	yellow
verde	green
anaranjado	orange
morado	purple
rosa, rosado	pink
negro	black
blanco	white
gris	grey
café, marrón, castaño (hair)	brown

LAS FORMAS GEOMETRICAS—Shapes

el círculo	circle
el semicírculo	semicircle
el cuadrado	square
el triángulo	triangle
el rectángulo	rectangle
el diamante	diamond
el óvalo	oval
la estrella	star
la línea	line

PROFESIONES—Professions

el maestro	teacher	
el jefe de la escuela	principal	
el ranchero	rancher	
el vaquero	cowboy	all masculine
el bombero	fireman	designations become
el cartero	mailman	feminine by changing
el policía	policeman	**el** to **la**
el enfermero	nurse	
el abogado	lawyer	endings in "-o"
el científico	scientist	become "-a"
el agricultor	farmer	
el pastor	minister	endings in "-or"
el doctor	doctor	become "-ora"
el, la dentista	dentist	
el, la deportista	athlete	endings in "-ista"
el periodista	reporter	do not change
el vendedor de.....	seller of....	
el dueño de....	owner of....	

LA FAMILIA—The Family

los padres	parents
la mamá, la madre	mother
el papá, el padre	father
el esposo	husband
la esposa	wife
la madrasta	step-mother
el padrasto	step-father
el hermano	brother
la hermana	sister
la niña, la muchacha	girl
el niño, el muchacho	boy
los niños, las niñas	children
la abuela	grandmother
el abuelo	grandfather
los bisabuelos	great-grandparents
el nieto, la nieta, los nietos	grandchildren
el primo, la prima (los primos)	cousin(s)
la tía	aunt

el tío	uncle
la sobrina	niece
el sobrino	nephew
los parientes	relatives (don't confuse w/ "parents")
la madrina	godmother
el padrino	godfather

PARTES DEL CUERPO—Parts of the Body

la cabeza	head	el pecho	chest
la cara	face	el estómago	stomach
los ojos	eyes	los brazos	arms
las cejas	eyebrows	el codo	elbow
las pestañas	eyelashes	las manos	hands
el pelo	hair	los dedos	fingers, toes
las orejas	ears	las uñas	nails
la boca	mouth	la cintura	waist
la nariz	nose	el trasero	bottom
la lengua	tongue	las piernas	legs
los dientes	teeth	las rodillas	knees
el cuello	neck	los pies	feet
la garganta	throat	la sangre	blood
la frente	forehead	el corazón	heart
las mejillas	cheeks	los huesos	bones
el hombro	back	los músculos	muscles
las espaldas	shoulders	la piel	skin

LA CLASE—The Classroom

la maestra / el maestro	teacher
los estudiantes, los alumnos, la clase	students
el escritorio	desk (teacher's)
el pupitre	desk (student's)
las sillas	chairs
los libros	books
el papel, los papeles	paper(s)
la puerta	door
la ventana	window
las luces	lights
la bandera	flag
la campana	bell

el suelo	floor
la pared	wall
la pizarra	chalkboard
la tiza	chalk
la pluma, el bolígrafo	pen
el borrador	eraser
el lápiz, los lápices	pencil(s)
el sacapuntos	sharpener
las tijeras	scissors
la pegadura	paste
el baño, el escusado	bathroom
la oficina	office
la biblioteca	library
la enfermera	nurse

LA ROPA—Clothing

la camisa	shirt
la camiseta	T-shirt
los pantalones	pants
los pantalones cortos	shorts
la blusa	blouse
el vestido	dress
los zapatos	shoes
el suéter, el abrigo	sweater
la falda	skirt
la chaqueta	jacket
el abrigo	coat
el rebozo	shawl
el cinturón	belt
los calcetines	socks

ANIMALES DOMESTICOS—Domestic Animals

el perro (la perra)	dog
el gato (la gata)	cat
el pez	fish
la tortuga	turtle
el pájaro	bird
el loro	parrot
el conejillo	guniea pig

ANIMALES DEL DESIERTO—Desert Animals

la víbora, la culebra, la serpiente	snake
el conejo	rabbit
el coyote	coyote
el puma	cougar
las ranas	frogs
el lagarto	lizard
el jabalí, la jabalina	javelina
la paloma	dove
el codorniz	quail
el correcaminos, el paisano	roadrunner

ANIMALES DEL RANCHO—Farm Animals

el caballo	horse
el burro	mule
la vaca	cow
la cabra	goat
la oveja	sheep
el cerdo, el cochinito	pig
el pato	duck
la gallina	hen
los pollitos	chickens
el gallo	rooster
el guajolote, el pavo	turkey

ANIMALES DEL ZOOLOGICO—Zoo Animals

el elefante	elephant
la jirafa	giraffe
el oso	bear
el tigre	tiger
el león	lion
la cebra	zebra
el venado	deer
los monos	monkeys
el gorila	gorilla
el hipopótamo	hippopotamus
animales en peligro de extinción	endangered animals

LA NATURALEZA—Nature

las montañas	mountains
el río	river
el desierto	desert
el bosque	forest
la selva pluvial, el bosque lluvioso	rain forest
el parque	park
los árboles	trees
la hierba	grass
las flores	flowers
las malas hierbas	weeds
el cacto	cactus
el lago	lake
el mar, el océano	ocean
la isla	island
el continente	continent
los campos	fields
el campo	countryside
la tierra	land
el arco iris	rainbow
la tormenta	storm
el aire	air
el viento	wind
la luna	moon
las estrellas	stars
el sol	sun
los planetas	planets
el espacio	space
el cometa	comet
el humo	smoke
la contaminación	pollution
el ambiente	environment
la conservación	conservation

APPENDIX C
Suggested Readings

EASY SPANISH BOOKS

Ada, Alma Flor. **La piñata vacía.** Illustrated by Vivi Escrivá. Compton, CA: Santillana Publishing Co., Inc., 1993.

Buchanan, Ken. **Esta casa está hecha de lodo**, This House Is Made of Mud. Illustrated by Libba Tracy. Flagstaff, AZ: Northland Publishing, 1991.

Charles, Donald. **El año de Gato Galano**, Calico Cat's Year. Illustrated by Donald Charles. Chicago: Children's Press, 1989.

Emberley, Rebecca. **My Day: a book in two languages**, Mi día: un libro en dos lenguas. Boston: Little, Brown, 1993.

Emberley, Rebecca. **Taking a Walk**, Caminando: A book in two languages. Boston, MA: Little, Brown, 1990.

Hall, Kirsten, and Jessica Flaxman. **¿Quién dice?** Illustrated by Wayne Becker. Chicago: Children's Press, 1990.

Krull, Kathleen. **María Molina and the Days of the Dead.** Illustrated by Enrique O. Sánchez. New York: Macmillan, 1994.

Matthias, Catherine. **Demasiados globos.** Illustrated by Gene Sharp. Chicago: Children's Press, 1990.

Mitchell, Marianne. **Doña Luna.** Illustrated by John Martinez Z. Littleton, MA: Sundance Publishing, 1995.

Mora, Pat. **The Desert Is My Mother,** El desierto es mi madre. Illustrated by Daniel Lechon. Houston, TX: Piñata Books, 1994.

Mora, Pat. **Listen to the Desert**, Oye al desierto. Illustrated by Francisco X. Mora. New York: Clarion Books, 1994.

Reiser, Lynn. **Margaret and Margarita**, Margarita y Margaret. New York: Greenwillow Books, 1993.

Tabor, Nancy. **Cincuenta en la cebra: contando con los animales**, Fifty on the zebra: counting with the animals. Watertown, MA: Charlesbridge Publishing, 1994.

Tripp, Valerie. **Pequeña Coala busca casa.** Illustrated by Sandra Cox Kalthoff. Chicago: Children's Press, 1989.

Wood, Audrey. **Veloz como el grillo.** Illustrated by Don Wood. Barcelona, New York: Child's Play (Spain), 1994.

MUSIC AND ACTIVITY BOOKS

Brady, Agnes M., and Margarita Márquez de Moats. **La Navidad: Christmas in Spain and Latin America.** Lincolnwood, IL: National Textbook Company, 1986.

Delacre, Lulu. **Arroz con leche: Popular Songs and Rhymes from Latin America.** Illustrated by Lulu Delacre. New York: Scholastic, 1989.

Linse, Barbara, and Richard Judd. **Fiesta! Mexico and Central America.** Carthage, IL: Feron Teacher Aids, 1993.

Orozco, José-Luis. **De Colores and Other Latin-American Folk Songs for Children.** New York: Dutton Children's Books, 1994.

Shalant, Phyllis. **Look What We've Brought You From Mexico.** Illustrated by Patricia Wayne. New York: Julian Messner, 1992.

Smith, Neraida. **Let's Sing and Learn in Spanish.** Lincolnwood, IL: Passport Books, 1992.

REFERENCE MATERIALS

Hammitt, Gene M. **Learn Spanish the Fast and Fun Way.** Hauppauge, NY: Barron's Educational Series, Inc., 1985.

Kendris, Christopher. **501 Spanish Verbs.** Woodbury, NY: Barron's Educational Series, Inc., 1982.

INDEX

ABOUT THE AUTHOR

Marianne Mitchell was born in Phoenix, Arizona, where she began her study of Spanish in the first grade. That early FLES (Foreign Language Program in Elementary School) program gave her a lifelong love of languages. She earned a B.A. degree in Spanish from the University of Redlands and her M.A. in Spanish from the University of Louisville.

Marianne has taught Spanish at all levels, from kindergarten through college. She has worked as a bilingual teacher in California, Idaho, and Arizona for several years. She currently conducts workshops for teachers trying to learn classroom Spanish.

Besides teaching, Marianne enjoys writing for children. Her stories and articles, in English and Spanish, have appeared in *Highlights for Children*, *New Moon*, *Skipping Stones*, *Mi Globo*, and other magazines. In 1995 she published her first book, *Maya Moon/Doña Luna*, with Sundance. It is a re-told folktale from Mexico explaining why the moon changes shape.

Marianne lives in Tucson, Arizona with her husband, Jim.

Heard About These Books.

from *Teacher Ideas Press*

COOKING UP WORLD HISTORY
Multicultural Recipes and Resources
Patricia C. Marden and Suzanne I. Barchers

This tasty resource allows you to take students on a culinary trip around the world! More than 20 countries and regions frequently studied in elementary and middle schools are represented. Each chapter has a description of the cookery of a culture, up to six recipes that provide a complete meal, research questions that connect the culture and food to history, and more. **Grades K–6.**
xv, 237p. 8½x11 paper ISBN 1-56308-116-4

MAGIC MINUTES
Quick Read-Alouds for Every Day
Pat Nelson

Guaranteed to spread a special magic over listeners and bring many minutes of enchantment to all, this collection of short stories (seasonally arranged) celebrates tried-and-true wisdom from around the world, as well as old-time humor and new-time heroes. **All Levels.**
xv, 151p. paper ISBN 0-87287-996-8

¡TEATRO!
Hispanic Plays for Young People
Angel Vigil

Actors and audience members experience and learn more about Hispanic culture and traditions of the American Southwest with these 14 reproducible scripts. **Grades 3–9.**
xviii, 169p. 8½x11 paper ISBN 1-56308-371-X

TRAVEL THE GLOBE
Multicultural Story Times
Desiree Webber, Dee Ann Corn, Elaine Harrod, Sandy Shropshire, and Donna Norvell

Go globe-trotting without ever leaving the classroom! This book recommends read-alouds and stories appropriate for flannel boards, overhead projections, or puppetry presentations. Songs, games, and simple crafts help your class navigate each international excursion. **Grades PreK–6.**
xxvii, 245p. 8½x11 paper ISBN 1-56308-501-1

THE CORN WOMAN
Stories and Legends of the Hispanic Southwest
Retold by Angel Vigil

The culture, history, and spirit of the Hispanic Southwest are brought to life through 45 *cuentos* (stories and legends) from the region. From ancient creation myths of the Aztecs and traditional tales of Spanish colonialists to an eclectic sampling of the work of modern Latino storytellers, this book provides a rich tapestry of tales—15 presented in both English *and* Spanish. **All levels.**
World Folklore Series
xxxi, 234p. color plates ISBN 1-56308-194-6

For a FREE catalog or to place an order, please contact:

Teacher Ideas Press
Dept. B9911 · P.O. Box 6633 · Englewood, CO 80155-6633
1-800-237-6124, ext. 1 · Fax: 303-220-8843 · E-mail: lu-books@lu.com

Check out our TIP Web site!
www.lu.com/tip